Marriageable
Alone Again but Not Alone

C in DYS

WESTBOW PRESS
A DIVISION OF THOMAS NELSON
& ZONDERVAN

Copyright © 2018 C in DYS.

All rights reserved. No part of this book may be used or reproduced by any means, graphic, electronic, or mechanical, including photocopying, recording, taping or by any information storage retrieval system without the written permission of the author except in the case of brief quotations embodied in critical articles and reviews.

Scripture quotations taken from the New American Standard Bible® (NASB), Copyright © 1960, 1962, 1963, 1968, 1971, 1972, 1973, 1975, 1977, 1995 by The Lockman Foundation Used by permission. www.Lockman.org

Interior Graphics/Art Credit: Michael Willett &Quinn Willett

WestBow Press books may be ordered through booksellers or by contacting:

WestBow Press
A Division of Thomas Nelson & Zondervan
1663 Liberty Drive
Bloomington, IN 47403
www.westbowpress.com
1 (866) 928-1240

Because of the dynamic nature of the Internet, any web addresses or links contained in this book may have changed since publication and may no longer be valid. The views expressed in this work are solely those of the author and do not necessarily reflect the views of the publisher, and the publisher hereby disclaims any responsibility for them.

Any people depicted in stock imagery provided by Thinkstock are models, and such images are being used for illustrative purposes only. Certain stock imagery © Thinkstock.

ISBN: 978-1-9736-1700-6 (sc)
ISBN: 978-1-9736-1699-3 (hc)
ISBN: 978-1-9736-1701-3 (e)

Library of Congress Control Number: 2018901468

Print information available on the last page.

WestBow Press rev. date: 04/18/2018

Contents

The tree of life 16

The sea of life 29

The truth in Life 58

marriage for life 131

This tree blossoms brightly, sweet perfume now abounds,
Love, Joy, peace, FRUITFULNESS! JOY TO ALL AROUND! 165

PART 1

Alone Again

An Island in a Calm and Tranquil Sea

When we are little, we are beautiful.
Life is a calm and tranquil sea.
When we are loved and happy;
Life, a dream, a game, a play,

Then the storms of life they rock us, it is hard for us to see
why troubles come and multiply, and spoil tranquillity.
Marriage may cause problems too that we did not then foresee.
As we do not agree with him or her; seems like conspiracy.
It wakes us up, we cannot sleep, and arguments arise
About some silliness, you see, and then we criticise.

You need
God's peace to rule your mind
And let peace over flow,
For He is love and joy and peace;
This fact you have to know.

Do not forget: with Christ within, your boat will never sink,
Nor waters overflow.

CInDys

Christ in Dyslexia
Christ in me
Christ in Thee
Christ is in everything you see.

Christ in,
The Movement of Birth .

See the miracle in movement that defies the mind of man,
As life flickers into being
may die,
because of sin.
Marriage may be a mountain,
Bickering,!
Despair.
It will die if we let it; the devil does n' t care.
So rise up and be counted!
Do not let the devil win.

Forgive,
Forgive
Forgive.
He says,
Holy Spirit help you win

You will rejoice, when marriage prospers,
Since Jesus loves His Church.
You have all - that is needed
to make your marriage work.
*He will give you peace and unity_*
He will bless your children too.
They'll grow to be believers,
Trust in Jesus just like you.

CInDys

<u>Christ *is* the Truth.</u> Truth must return

"What is truth?" the preacher said.
Is it in the heart or in the head?
See in every bird and every tree,
Little whiskers peeping out,
Telling us our God's about.

CInDys

Christ in,
Relationships

The more times our Christian relationships are divided and torn apart-, the weaker we become as individuals and as a body of believers- In order to remedy this fact, we need to understand what repentance really means for us as individuals and as a body of believers.

A very important question is why there are so many honest followers of the Lord *Jesus left 'Alone Again'.*

Such divisiveness in marriages, devastate the local church, and its effects spread like poison throughout the church as a whole.

The intention here is to put a stop to these divisions in the Body of Christ using,

<u>The Bible,</u>
<u>*The Sword of the Spirit.*</u>

Christ in,
Our story

The surrounding churches are baffled.
They thought the blessed marriage would last.
Then one by one,
Others, would tumble
Till marriage itself is a farce,
Broken lives and families,
Marriage, a thing of the past.
Who is my real father or mother?'
On Father God, I am cast.
But at times, God you look, like my father,
angry and violent and tough.

He runs away when it suits him,
Shouting, he's had enough!

But, somehow I always will love him.
God's found him a place in my heart.
Forgive him, forgive him, my heart says.
Yes, I've been forgiven enough.
I want to see him in heaven
at the end of life's journey, so rough.
Then we'll sing together with angels,
our problems a thing of the past.

CInDys

Christ dismisses,

Pride

What is Pride?
the preacher said.
In the eyes,
or in the head?

It's in the ones who often sing,
"I'm the greatest, I'm the king."
Pride is a form of lust we know.
Lust
kills the spirit.
It must go!
Yes, lust is hungry,
It loves itself,
Looks for pleasure
everywhere.
For the other
Does not care,
Wastes its substance,
Wastes its time,
Does not seek to walk the line
of fidelity.

Alone but Not Alone

Remember God is with you
On that lonely road you take.
He'll never leave you
Nor forsake.
He'll give good gifts;
He'll not take.
He'll give you strength
To endure it,
Strength and help
Endure the pain.
The pruning process is so hurtful.
As it comes and comes again,
You may shout and call for
Mercy
.Christ knows what you're going through.
He suffered and He died to help you.
Good fruit will soon appear in you.

CInDys

MARRIAGEABLE ALONE AGAIN BUT NOT ALONE

Christ, on the long road Home

The road is long and lonely;
We cannot see the end.
We try to see around the bend,
Trees, obscure our view.
The trees are sometimes fruitful,
But, now, they're dead and bare.
They must be pruned, and cherished.
God's discipline is fair.

CInDys

Living together, unwed.

You told him you would live together,
marriage a thing of the past
since too many friends and family,
relationships end in divorce.
You think you are safer together
*<u>**without**</u> the marriage vows,*
so you plod on through life's dilemmas,
nothing to help love stay fast.

It's not marriage that is the problem.
Marriage is fine for all.
but a marriage without commitment
brings sorrow, to all at the last.

You'll be teaching your child
through your actions
that nothing's important in life,
not even the love and devotion
of a man for his well-loved wife.
You're less likely to grow old together,
less likely to overcome strife.
Divorce is not the problem,
but commitment to a partner for life.
If you both make your vows together
before the King of all Kings,
He'll help you to keep them forever,
an example for your kids.
Because others were not obedient,
need not be a problem for you.

CInDys

Look at couples who've overcome problems,
the problems that ensue.

A marriage of love and obedience
is more likely to endure.
Better be single and lonely
than be married to someone untrue.

A person who'll love you and leave you,
and go after somebody new,
Leave you to cope with the children.
(Faithful believers are few.)

CInDys

A sad song from the past

Oh, sad is the fortune of all woman kind,
She's always restricted, she's always confined,
Confined by her parents until she's a wife,
A slave to her husband,
for the rest of her life.
I'm just a poor girl, and my future is set.
I've always been courted, by the wagoner's lad ;
He's courted me daily, by night and by day, and
now he is leaving and going away.

This old song reflects the fact that living together does not mean that couples *stay* together. Marriage was encouraged by the Christian church to protect women and their children from exploitation.

A Single Woman's Solace

"When I'm tempted to repine,
Bemoan my single lot,
I sit right down,
and make a list
of the men
whose wife
I'm glad I'm not".

- Author unknown –

Temptation
What the bible says

"There is no temptation taken you, but that which is common to man, but God is faithful and just and will not suffer us to be tempted beyond our ability to overcome and with the temptation will also provide a way of escape so we can endure it."
(1Corinthians10:13).

"Then the Lord knows how to rescue the godly from temptation."
(2 peter 2:9)

Beware the roots of bitterness

The tree of life

Here we have a couple.
In a trap they're caught.
The sadness of their background
into their minds has wrought
a heaviness and loneliness,
a trap, in which they're caught.

Their life is full of sadness now.
Though songs of love
They sought,
Instead, there're groans of misery;
in tragedy they're caught.

CInDys

Chapter 1

We hear every day of young men who walk out on their marriages or partners, giving the reason that they are tired of being married. This probably means they are tired of the responsibility marriage brings. Yet who can honestly say that he or she would not like a faithful spouse who will be faithful until death parts them, as the old marriage promise emphasizes?

I truly believe, that it's the Church's responsibility to point people back to biblical norms, which would make a depth of commitment possible in all our lives.

Teaching about depth of commitment, could also be a guideline that includes proactive teams within the Church and its ministry. The church needs to minister to troubled marriages

Christ overcame temptation.

<u>Our friendships should remain *in Christ.*</u>

We should not be hypersensitive, because we are the body of Christ on earth. We should learn to confront relational problems early on.

If we let difficulties fester, or if we harbour grudges, we will increase our own pain, and the dispute will get out of proportion, hindering the progress of *any* kind of relationship.

Marriage is a special relationship and aims to be the epitome of a Christ centred, loving and forgiving relationship with His people the Church.

Forgiveness, therefore, must be the watchword of a successful marriage and should be even more so if we intend to embark on a second marriage.

We must look to Jesus, if we want to succeed!

<u>Christ in,</u>
<u>Success</u>

<u>The trap breaks.</u>
The trap will soon be broken
when they to Jesus turn.
He'll bring them back together
Since, for unity they yearn.
Dark days may be before them,
But the storm will soon be past.
The love of God unites them,
as on Him they both are cast.

CInDys

Questions and Answers.

1. Who is marriageable after a divorce?
2. Should I remarry after a divorce?

-It depends on why you want to marry again-

1. Was it you or your partner who broke the marriage vows?

And are you healed from the effects of the first relationship?

It may depend on how long you had been married.

If it was your partner who was the aggressive one (the divorcer), was it because he or she was lusting after someone else and refused to change direction or repent, as the Bible puts it?

Repent is a military term that means **"about turn."** You are going in one direction, and at the captain's command, you must turn in the opposite direction.

You need to turn away from sin and exercise practical love and self-control. Jesus said, "Deny yourself." Take up your cross and follow Him. He'll give you strength to remain celibate, if that's the only way for you because you are gay.

Some practical suggestions for married people in troubled situations include the following.

- Go on holiday together and decide what went wrong.
- Find a church that offers marriage-enrichment classes.
- Find a mentor family that has overcome problems similar to your own.

Many marriages break up because of financial disagreements. Before the marriage is in crisis, do the following.

- Set up a joint account.
- Agree on individual spending money.

You may need to *both* cut out nonessentials.

Find agreement regarding spending money. Spending money may include children's pocket money. You may need a mentor to chair the first meeting about money.

Who Leads

It is the husband, who is the "head" of the wife according to the bible, although often a mentor will need to help with especially difficult decisions. He or she will need to act as a chair person.

This does not mean he is the boss. That is Jesus Himself, and His sheep need to hear His voice, which involves *listening to both sides of the problem.* But remember, that although Jesus was the servant King, no one treated Him like an odd-job man, as wives sometimes do with their husbands. Neither should, a wife be treated as a skivvy, being ordered to do the nasty jobs no one else wants to do. Children should not be exasperated in this way either. We are all heirs together of grace and compassion.

Adultery

This is the downfall of many marriages today.

Avoid pornography like the plague.

Watch movies that encourage Christian family values. (Larry Levenson produces many such films.) If you have children, monitor them when they are online. If they go to friends' homes, keep in close touch with the parents.

We are living in days when there is a terrible, deadly war to take over the minds and hearts of our children. We as parents must do our very best to overcome this evil intervention by applying the good news contained in the Bible.

Drastic measures are needed in cases of adultery, such as moving house or changing jobs away from temptation. This pattern will not be broken without constant personal discipline and forgiveness.

Some testimonies

A Young Man's Recent Journey

Below is the testimony of a man who recently overcame the rejection of divorce – through church intervention and the power of the Holy Spirit.-

I was not, brought up to attend church. I left because of one bad experience: the death of my father. I drifted into a marriage with a nonbeliever who became severely unfaithful to me, and I felt I had to leave the district where we had lived and had children together.

As I said, I was forced to move house because of my divorce situation, but this in the end proved to be a God-directed move. I eventually met a trainee pastor from a local church who invited me to attend her church. After much thought, I did attend and ended up recommitting my life to Jesus.

Even though I had constantly asked myself, "Do I really want to start that again?" I had also thought about where I was. I was lonely, had nothing to do, and had no friends in this new town and county where I had moved three months earlier.

I then asked myself, "What do I have to lose?' If I did not like the new church, I simply would not go back.

As I walked toward the door, I remember thinking;

"Will the next three minutes be the same, or will it be a life changer?" I prayed to God, "Please let the next three minutes change my life."

My goodness, He did not disappoint! I was welcomed by the lady whom I had met a couple of weeks before. She said, "Come and sit with us." The vicar and a few others came to welcome me. God's timing was perfect.

The very next evening, the church was starting the Alpha course, and I was invited. I went to Alpha week one. Each week, we covered a new subject. By the end of the course, I was going to the church regularly.

But my faith was severely tested at this time. I was told, by my employer that my role was being made redundant. I could not help myself. I asked God why. But even though this was a major disaster to me, and my newfound faith was severely put to the test, God resolved all these problems. I became more successful in my job than before. My mortgage problems were resolved, and I developed good relationships in the church. In retrospect, I remember that during the Holy Spirit Day of the Alpha course, one of the leaders took me to one side to encourage me personally. She said, "Unfailing love, doors will be open. Trust God"

All this, however, happened while looming court action from my divorce was approaching. I started handing over my life to Jesus on a daily basis. God has taken me on a path in the past three years with all sorts of challenges and obstacles, and He has helped me to overcome some real difficult situations. He has been with me every step of the way.

The court case was a nightmare experience, but I felt the Holy Spirit's presence coming alongside me with the prompting, "Stay firm to the truth." I did, and truth prevailed. The final settlement was fair.

My work life totally changed. I was in a new branch, which was a much better place to work. The marriage debts were sorted with my mortgage demands. My relationship with my children grew even stronger.

Another prompting came to me. "Don't look at the things you don't have, but be grateful for the things you do have."

I'm praising Him every day. I am involved in youth leadership now and the church music band, which is a wonderful way of worshiping the Lord, who is helping me so much.

Things have really been working together for my good as the bible says

The Bible answers the aloneness that comes after an unsuccessful marriage, including how to decide if we are ready to remarry. It also includes how we can maintain unity in the home, especially when two homes and two families of children are involved.

Chapter 2

How do we remain on the solid foundation, which is Jesus Christ?

The sea of life

Christ in,
Contemplation

A Man Standing Alone

I am standing all alone;
looking out to sea.
I think about my marriage
and the things that ought to be.

I think about our arguments.
Why did she so blame me,
While I was only trying, to
understand n' then agree.
Because I'm not a woman
and want to put it right,
I try to see her point of view;
but, then we always fight.
We go back into history
To find out who was right.
And if the truth were only seen,
Only prayer can put it right.
I cry unto our Father God.
Yes, He can put it right.
I fight the anger, not my wife;
Then God will put it right.

CInDys

Our prayer guide

Our Father
Which art in heaven,
May Your name be
Revered,
in all the earth.
Bring Your heaven to earth.
May Your love fill our lives and
our marriages.
May we stay together,
As we pray together,
And, obey Your teaching at all times,

-A free interpretation of part of the Lord's prayer-

<u>CInDys</u>

Christ in, you

Jesus said,
I will forgive you, but only
As you forgive others from your heart.

Write a list of things you need to forgive.
I forgive you for blaming me,
though it was not my fault.

I forgive you for _____.

I forgive myself for _____.

"I can do all things through Christ who strengthens me." (Phil. 4:13),

Our Prayer continued.

May Your will be done,
on earth as in heaven.
Give us this day our daily bread
And forgive us our debts
As we forgive our debtors.
Lead us not into temptation,
But deliver us from evil,
For thine is the kingdom
The power and the glory for ever.

You Lord God, make our marriages work.

LOVE

Love, is the greatest spiritual gift and should
be at the base of Christian marriage.
**Without love, we are just like a harsh noisy instrument. Love
surpasses other spiritual gifts and goes on eternally.
(1 Corinthians 1-30)**

"Without God (His love), there is nothing!" My grandma spoke these words not long before she died of cancer.

(I was sixteen at the time, and had recently asked her if she knew Jesus as her Saviour). She has certainly passed on her faith on to me.

Chapter 3

Our genetic make - up, is programmed by our background experience. We hear this, through the language we use when talking to our children. As my family have grown up, I have noticed that they tend to use the very words and phrases we used to them as parents, especially when disciplining or being angry with our children

Family life can bring out the best or worst in us.

Love needs to be the foundation of our marriages.

Love heals.

Love helps us to find healing, from our painful childhood memories, and then we can pass on this healing to our offspring.

We need to be honest with one another about our weaknesses, and we should confess and admit, we have God-given strengths.

These might *even* have stemmed from past privations that our loving Father in heaven has worked together for good. We all have a choice in these matters.

On one hand, we may decide to linger in feelings of self-pity, blaming ourselves, or others, for our distress and thus becoming irreversibly bitter; on the other hand, with God's enabling, we can repent of bitterness and allow the trial to make us better and more useful people, helping others to overcome similar problems. All things do work together for good for those who love God; the called, according to **His** purposes. What we must *not* do is give up the struggle and escape into a world of alcohol and hypnotic drugs, as certain people I have read about have done.

Prescription drugs and painkillers seem to be a fashionable escape route today, and we *need prayer*, to overcome and to get out of these habits.

We need to seek help from people who understand our needs and preferably have overcome similar problems themselves.

It may be true that in some cases, of depression, or bipolar, that wrong use of drugs, may have brought us to near suicide, but there is **always** help in Jesus .

He will answer the cry of faith, also, once we have been healed, Jesus can also lead us to help others to overcome, even clinical depression and its aftermath as we follow Jesus closely.

Jesus' healing, through faithful relationships.

In many cases, the love of a good husband, wife, and family, bring healing and enable visions of future and even present success. Emotional healing from past failures can be part of this.

Christ in,
What we read

I enjoy reading about people who have overcome in life, against great odds. I am trying to understand my own reactions. and also compare them with the lives of people of past and present, who have found ways of using life's experiences to move forward rather than allowing themselves to drift back into despair. I have noticed in many of the biographies, and especially in my experiences, that people usually need an impetus, outside themselves to keep them focussed on a goal.

John Newton is a good example of a life that eventually focussed on Jesus.
He was the author of the timeless hymn, 'Amazing Grace'.

It was God's grace and mercy during his terrible seafaring history that had led him into the slave trade, which affected Him so profoundly. God used his faithful fiancée, Polly, to help him return to the Lord after he had backslidden so badly. He thought of her, all alone and waiting patiently for him to return and no doubt, was part of why his life was transformed.

John never forgot Polly, who had waited for him so patiently through all his seafaring and womanising escapades. Eventually, he married her and they made an excellent team together. He then became an amazing, faithful husband and pastor, and wrote, "Amazing grace, how sweet the sound, that saved a wretch like me, I once was lost but now am found, was blind but now I see." Faith in the Lord Jesus and a faithful wife made all the difference. He became a faithful and devoted husband and pastor.

John Newton also had had a good mother who died young. I am sure her prayers had a great deal to do with his transformation.

He had followed his father's footsteps when he went to sea but once there, he kicked over the traces in every way possible, as many young men do.

Although he did not know it, this may have been for the excitement and the adrenalin rush it produced. Rebellion and frustration seem to go hand in hand.

However, the Bible points out, rebellion is like the sin of witchcraft: it grows from a bitter root that needs pulling out, right at the start.

I wonder what the result would have been had Polly left her husband for another man at any stage.

She, however, lived in a different era from ours, when the woman in particular, was expected to be the faithful one in a relationship, while the man sowed his wild oats.

Polly probably did not know or want to know, what was going on in John Newton's life while he was away at sea.

Chapter 4

Life after Divorce

In this section, I am thinking about the subject of life after divorce and trying to observe, what makes a person marriageable after a divorce.

It seems clear to me that a person, who has been through a terrible childhood, may recover from the effects of a disastrous background through an excellent and loving marriage; he or she will then become marriageable.

Survival of a troubled marriage

If a marriage is to survive, practical love must be there and at least one member of the partnership needs to be a balanced and whole person. In many cases, the troubled person may reciprocate that love, although to begin with, he or she may find it almost impossible to express loving feelings. He or she will need God's help in this circumstance.

God is love, and He has feelings. Jesus wept at tomb of His friend Lazarus.

The question I am still seeking to answer now, however, is how a person who has been rejected all-round, can recover in a biblical way.

From my own experience, reflecting on the fact that Jesus was a man of sorrows and rejected by all his friends several times, was a great help. He promised to be the Father of the widows and fatherless.

I considered myself a spiritual war widow, and Father God had promised to be the father of people in my situation.

Christ in, Rejection

You think you have been rejected,
and everyone is mean;
that the people you befriended
were enemies unseen.
You did them good and helped them,
prayed for them – it's true.
But behind your back, they gossiped,
and your reputation slew.

But *you must* forgive them.
They know not what they do.
Jesus said forgive them
like He's forgiven you.

CInDys

Summary

Alone Again but Marriageable, covers various aspects of relationships, taking the position that our marital relationships must affect and include relating to one another in a healthy way from birth to death. All relationships including platonic ones, affect not only us as individuals, but also, our relatives and future generations. Jesus showed us the way to give love and kindness in a practical way. His kind of love never fails, and if we have His Holy Spirit, He will make any one of us truly marriageable, even if we remain single for the rest of our lives.

In this work, I have called people who break up homes and legal, Christ,- Centred marriages, Divorcers.
Unfortunately, today, anything goes and masquerades as marriage.

Men pretend to be married to other men, and women to other women. Famous people even boast about having had children by a surrogate mother. No way, is God the author of such unnatural confusion.

Even Christians give lip service to this parody of family life, as they try to accommodate gay couples in their buildings.

The homosexual in the church.

This does *not* mean that genuine churches should not entertain homosexual people and help them get deliverance.

I have heard however, that some secular authorities have closed down Christian counselling organisations, where homosexuals have sought and found help.

The grounds secular organisations give for doing this is that they think homosexuality is normal and does not need help.

We have strayed such a long way from Bible teaching. The Apostle Paul, in Romans chapter 1, says that in the last days, men will burn in their lust towards one another.

Women will be used and use one another unnaturally as well. The end of all this will be that God will give them up to depravity.

Such people, like Jezebel of old, will reach a point when they are beyond help and *cannot* repent.

(Jezebel, and her lovers, had to be thrown out, and their sin destroyed, in order for her adulteries to be terminated.) In the Old Testament, the main way to terminate pagan practices was to destroy the idol worshippers and their cult prostitutes together, through literal warfare.

We need to do this through prayerful, spiritual warfare, which should transform lives and is therefore much more desirable. The famous picture of Jezebel thrown to the dogs for her wickedness, horrendous though it is, is not even comparable to the fires of hell prepared for the devil and all those who follow him to destruction.

> How can we escape if we neglect the great
> salvation offered us in Christ Jesus!
>
> The Lord Jesus did such a wonderful thing when
> He shed His blood for *all* people.
>
> There is no sin He cannot blot out while we are
> alive. But after that the judgement.

Whatever our sins or problems, He can give us a new start.

We do have *free will* however, and we have to let the Holy Spirit do His work of renewal of our mind set.

However, the Church has one important task: that of rescuing repentant homosexuals and couples who are committing adultery.

It is the Church's job to help <u>repentant</u> divorcers find acceptance in Christ. The world will always try to stop its followers from repenting, and it will find various ways of excusing and promoting sin. We are told not to love the world or the things within the world", and that includes its attitudes to sin. If we do so, the love of God is not in us (1. John 2:15)

People who are in constant sin, and are part of the Church, *do* need the ministry of deliverance. If they repent from their sin, be it adultery or homosexuality, we need to give them *healthy* companionship in a prayer and Bible study group that can help them to overcome their temptations.

This means that we hate the sin but love the sinner, and we seek to rescue him or her from the way that leads to death.

We all have the responsibility of leading new believers into Christ's forgiveness and helping them to see that Christ can help them overcome on a permanent basis.

Christ in, Children

Child hood is the most effective time for people to learn bible truth.

Parents and teachers have a wonderful opportunity to influence young lives while they are young and untouched by worldly errors.

We are told in Proverbs, to train up a child while he is young, and when he is old, he will not depart from it,

When I contact elderly people I can see, how strongly their childhood memories influence their lives today.

I remember the songs taught by an elderly Sunday School teacher when I was five years old, the song still helps me. "Loving shepherd of thy sheep, keep thy lamb in safety keep. Nothing can thy power withstand, none can pluck me from Thy hand."

I have heard many people of all ages say they were taught the Lord's Prayer when they were children at school, and they have never forgotten it.

Ian McCormack-often referred to as 'the jellyfish man'- is one example of the importance of praying the contents of the Lord's prayer-(He was stung by several deadly boxer jelly- fish and died as a result)

He testifies- all over the world now- that he quoted the Lord's Prayer in the ambulance while he was being rushed to the hospital; that prayer, was answered in a spectacular way, and he was given a vision of Jesus, who showed him the horrors of hell and the joys of heaven.

After he repented of his evil ways, Jesus gave him the choice, of either going to heaven there and then, or he could return to life on earth. Ian decided to return to earth. He was certified as dead later, and his body was sent to the mortuary.

It was in the mortuary that God brought him back to life, which filled the mortuary attendants with terror, as one can imagine.

How sad that many schools no longer promote Bible-based assemblies! Parents so rarely teach their children to pray, or even to thank God for food at mealtimes.

As said before, Ian learnt the Lord's Prayer at his mother's knee, and Jesus spoke to him in the ambulance, giving him visions of the fires of hell and the joys of heaven. When given the choice, he chose to come back to this world because he did not want to die, leaving his mother to think that he had died without knowing Christ as his Saviour.

May more mothers begin teaching their children to pray!

Train up a child in the way he should go, and when he is old, he will not depart from it. However, we must make sure the teaching is biblically sound.

Chapter 5

Non-Christian Partners

Biblically, there may be good reasons for a man to divorce his wife, or even for a woman to divorce her husband, although the latter was extremely difficult in Old Testament times because wives were considered, **the husband's property – a household slave, we might say today-**

Non- believing wives

In the book of an Old Testament prophet called Ezra, we find that he was extremely angry because so many men had forgotten God's express teaching on the subject of marriage and had married heathen wives. He pointed out that even Solomon, the wisest man on earth, had fallen away from his faith in the living God and worshipped the idols of the various women he had married. With great severity, Ezra commanded Israel to divorce their foreign idol worshipping wives, even though they had had children by them. This was a clear commandment from God, and it would seem better to divorce a pagan spouse than fall away from the God of our salvation.

Paul taught that if non-believing partners **wanted** to leave, to let them go, but if they chose to stay; spouses should try to win the pagan man or woman to Christ, *through Christ-like behaviour.*

Jesus taught that to divorce a spouse for any cause more trivial than pornographic sin, or sexual filth, such as adultery, was totally, unacceptable, and **to remarry, would also involve the new partner, in an adulterous relationship.**

Divisive divorcers should not remarry and spread the rot. They needed to clearly repent and resolve issues with their previous lawful partners.

The first lesson here is that we should be doubly careful that we allow our Saviour Jesus to lead us in choosing a life partner.

We must be careful of people who attend church before the wedding, for hypocritical reasons (I have heard of several people who thought they were marrying a genuine Christian, only to find after the ceremony that the partner was into New Age philosophy, or even Buddhism, which denies the saving work of Christ.) Satan is very good at blinding our eyes. I cannot count, how many men in particular, who promised to go to church before the wedding but then did not go near a church afterwards.

I truly believe now, that it may be necessary to divorce a wayward partner if he refuses to repent and turn to Christ, especially if the Christian spouse is moving towards denying her own faith in Jesus.

Leaders need to do all in their power to help. He or she must make sure that the next partner is a genuine believer.

The underlying belief I have often heard expressed, is that the individual might get converted *after* the marriage. This rarely happens in real life. It cannot be emphasised enough that we make sure that the marital partner is a genuine believer.

Pre-marital counselling is a good idea in most cases, and through prayer and Bible knowledge, couples should be able to resolve this problem.

Most likely, the wayward divorcer partner was not ready for marriage in the first place. Some divorcers *do* repent, but this must mean that they "about turn" and turn to Jesus, who makes us whole, marriageable people.

Marriage in the New Testament is a picture of, Christ's relationship with His Church. It is no wonder Satan does all in his power to destroy marriages, and subsequently family life and structure.

Let us unite as a body of believers, tear down his strongholds, and bring the marriages together in Jesus's love.

Leaders

Leaders in the church need to admit their past mistakes to the people and families they are mentoring. They also need to emphasize how they overcame or proposed to overcome these problems in a biblical way.

The church is sick inside because so many marriages have failed during the last ten to twenty years, even amongst leaders, and church members have followed the landslide. The problem is not divorce itself. The prophet told people to divorce themselves from non-believing, rebellious wives, even if they had fathered children by them. Our *non-Christian* relationships are an attack of darkness to make us lose faith in Jesus. God must come first.

Even Solomon, the wisest man on earth, made this mistake hundreds of times, and it caused his downfall at the end of his life. It's important to begin well, but it's even more important to end well. Self-control is essential in spiritual warfare.

The Apostle Paul, who had overcome so much opposition from other people, enemies and friends alike, had no confidence in his own flesh. He stated clearly, "I keep my body under control, in case I, having preached to others, I myself become a castaway" (1 Cor. 9:27).

Pastor David Instone-Brewer

A book written by David Instone-Brewer, *Divorce and Remarriage in the Church*, has been instrumental in helping me and others understand biblical teachings on divorce from a point of view different from the norm.

David Instone-Brewer explains how rampant divorce was in Israel in Biblical times, and this is why Jesus made it clear that "any cause" divorces were not acceptable in God's sight. Moses allowed them because men had "hard hearts", according to the Lord Jesus.

As a pastor, David Instone-Brewer refused to marry individuals who were leaving faithful relationships in order to marry someone else. On the other hand, he *would* marry divorcees who were remarrying after being let down by a former spouse. Even with these, he would get them together as far as possible with the former spouse and prospective new partner, ensuring that forgiveness was all-round. I am sure this would involve acknowledging and the rooting out any kind of bitterness.

I have examined my own life while reading and studying the Bible, and I find it strengthens me every day and helps me examine my heart and root out, any root of bitterness there that might choke the fruit of the Holy Spirit from growing in me.

My watchword is, "They that wait on the Lord renew their strength."

Christ in,
the gift of a child

My life is like
A little light
That flickers into flame.
My life is like a battery:
Some good, some bad, some tame.

Your life may be
A useful thing.
Don't treat it like a game.
For the moments fly,
And all you do
May only die with you.

CInDys

Christ in, Movement

There's a miracle in movement
That defies the mind of man.
As life flickers into being,
Only dies because of sin.
Our marriages may be mountains
of bickering despair;
They will die if we let them.
The devil doesn't care.

So rise up and be counted!
Don't let the devil win.
Forgive, forgive, forgive.
Then the Holy Spirit helps you win.

CInDys

Christ in,
My Story

My life is like a little light that flickers into flame.
It lives and glows and grows and dies, surrounded by the pain.
I toddle into childhood.
My parents think I'm great –
Until they see that now I know their love has turned to hate.

They fight and scrap and criticise, but they can't really see
That all their hurt and anger really falls on me.
The childish trust God put in me,
Since children are His love,
Is flickering now
And burning low.
"Sorry" comes too late.

As I grow and look around, and teenage looms ahead,
I hear the devil's laughter: "Your mother wished you dead."

I go to church, and there I find others just like me.
They're blind to love, brought up with hate.
They're blind and deaf like me.

I listen to the radio.
A man speaks to my heart.
He says he'll read the Bible from the very start.
Since people don't obey it,
Doesn't mean it isn't true.
It must have a message for me and then for you.

CInDys

A page a day is what he says his resolution is,
So I will give my time to this and see if it is true.
I read it with an open mind, trying to obey.
I feel that I am so very bad (this is what they say).

I come to Revelation,
And fear fills me with despair.
Until I hear the words of Christ:
"Come and do not doubt."

I come to Him just as I am,
Weary and worn and sad.
In Him I've found a resting place,
And He has made me glad.
He's helped me through the storms of life,
All its ups and downs.

Through divorce and marriage,
because His love is true.

So for this I want to say though the flame of life may die,
Christ's own love that fills me now
Will grow and never die,

CInDys

Christ in,
Our Journey
Abroad.

We travelled to the mountains;
We felt we had to go!
Though we had two baby daughters
Following us, I know.
All our friends and family
Cried, "You shouldn't go!"
And so
When things went wrong,
We returned in shame,
But the Saviour helped us through.
Through the pain
Of shattered dreams,
Sickness, and failure too.

He heals the broken-hearted
And binds up their many wounds.
The battle will soon be over.
Victory is in view.

CInDys

A tree, behind a solid wall of protection.

The truth in Life

Christ in,
Our life abroad

I worked with my then husband and two infant daughters, and I saw the miraculous birth of our two sons there, in that difficult situation. I think I should share to some degree how difficult it was for others working in that situation too. Medical facilities were sadly lacking at that time, and there was only one doctor who had had some training abroad. He had to cover all medical needs over a vast area.

When I became pregnant with my first son, we had to make difficult decisions. We had to choose a home birth and trust the doctor would help us in time, or travel two days to the city in order to give birth there.

This latter solution would involve different dangers and there was the problem of lodgings.

There was the question too, would the child's heart stand the vast change in altitude?

Our home birth option would involve a deep trust in God, and trust that we would get the needed medical help in time if there were an emergency – which there certainly was!

There *was* another option, to travel what could be two days to a clinic in the altitude, but this journey would be long and even more hazardous than the city option, along narrow roads with death trap precipices on either side. We made this journey for the birth of our second son, but we decided on a home birth for our first son.

Overcoming Fear

I constantly prayed against fear attacks during both pregnancies.

I had at that time, heard of a neighbour who had died in childbirth on the way to the city.

I heard about this sad event at the same time as one of my pregnancies.

She and her husband had decided to travel to the city for the wife to have her baby. Sadly, the mother and baby died on the way. You can imagine the fears I went through at this time!

I could only pray with all my heart, for strength and peace, to overcome these fears, because fear is the main foothold that Satan, uses to work against faith.

I can only guess why the other woman lost her baby and her own life. But I can give my own testimony here about how the Lord has been better than a doctor or a husband to me through these traumas, especially through the later trauma of divorce.

Christ in, new birth

You Saw Me

You saw me through that difficult birth.

I seemed to be travelling from heaven to earth.

You saw me there

When all seemed lost,
When sons were born at such great cost
All through the pains and trials of life.
Though not my own, you saved my life.
You lost your life to give back mine.
You saw me through your love divine.
Yours is the love that lasts through death,
Till glory takes away our breath.
Death where is thy sting,
Your blood has washed away my sin.
You see me.

CInDys

Christ in,
Our emergencies.

My husband at the time, and I went through a great deal together in those days. We had to stay prayerful and close to God and His Word in order to survive.

How we prayed during that journey for the birth of our fourth child.

The birth was imminent all through that journey. Even now, so many years later, I wonder at the way God sustained us as labour pains continued all through that journey.

We would stop and pray each time a pain came, and about an hour before we arrived at the clinic, the placenta began to come away. I think only the medically inclined will realize how perilous this situation was for both me, and the unborn child.

God preserved us in His most wonderful way as we prayed and agreed together. Agreeing prayer is essential in every situation.

We travelled in pitch darkness for a good part of what proved to be a two-day journey in a truck, with our other three children trying to sleep *at times* in the back, sometimes finding breathing difficult as we travelled higher still.

All we could see, as we travelled along those winding, treacherous tracks, were scattered buses and cars that had rolled down the precipices from time to time. Later, we saw the lights of tiny hamlets as pitch darkness fell.

As I said earlier, we would stop and pray as intermittent labour pains came. I lost count of how many times we did this, with one emergency after another, until the most faith-provoking one of all.

If only we had continued to pray with such fervency throughout our married life!

The powers of darkness did their worst to ruin our marriage.

The doctor and nurse who attended me, for the birth of our youngest child, affirmed, it was the hand of Father God who prevented our suffering the same fate as the neighbour and her baby.

All I can say is God takes us home when He knows we are ready. The judge of all the earth always does right, and He allows our homecoming at certain times for reasons we do not understand now, but we will understand one day, looking at life from God's perspective.

In any case, we know He wants the best for us. He cares for us as we trust in Him alone, and His timing is perfect, whether it's good or bad from our point of view.

Chapter 5

Christ in,
Life as a Divorcee

I have read several books written by divorcees, and others written to minister into divorce situations. One written by Pastor David Instone-Brewer, was very helpful, dealing with divorced couples, especially those who belong to the Church. I have found it necessary to differentiate between the aggressor, or divisive person by referring to the divisive person as a ***divorcer.***

I have concluded that there is a clear biblical distinction between a divorcee and a divorcer.

David, as a pastor, had to resolve many complicated situations. Between divorcees, and divorcers. The divorcer would be the divisive person in a marriage breakup. (He or she may even be someone outside the marriage.)

We need "discernment of spirits" as a Church, when the seeds of divorce creep into our marriages.

Christ in, My Background

In my case, my father was not a practicing believer, so there was no church to help in order for my parents to avoid divorce, or even want to.

In Christian marriage, the seeds of divorce can be very subtle and come in many disguises, even at the beginning of our relationships.

We are all responsible for our own thought life, it's no use being in denial about other people and what they are up to, especially in marital matters. This must include what is happening in the lives of our spouses.

I believe that we should fight to keep our marriages together, and if necessary, we should not be too proud to seek the Church's help.

The disaster of acrimonious divorce is a terrible thing and it should only be a last resort. In a sense, if we were married in the Church, it is the Church's responsibility to help us rescue this vital church relationship, or even where the divorcer is intransigent, pronounce the marriage irretrievably broken down. The reason can only be unrepentant adultery porno, or in other words, sexual filth or violence, which according to Jesus is the root of murder.

The foundation of prayer

United prayer based on obedience and agreement is essential in God's work. Although we were, blessed, financially and were able to purchase three to four houses for our work, the foundation of the work was shaky.

Prayer needs to be honest and sincere and in agreement with The Word of God. This is difficult if one partner has an eye on divorce. Both partners and the prayer warriors need to be fighting the fight of faith on behalf of the marriage. Leadership marriages will always be under threat, and all concerned need to be determined to pray for the marriage to work and healing to take place where needed.

When we all pray, we need to be sure that our hearts are pure. We need to remember, "If I regard iniquity in my heart, the Lord will not hear me."

For lack of united prayer and many other reasons, my marriage ended in divorce. I fought hard to keep the marriage together, apologising to those involved for my part in the marriage breakdown. This was taken to be, a confession of my guilt (which had been gossiped around already). That is why I emphasize here that the *real,* truth *must* be found regarding marital issues.

It was about this time more than ten years ago that I have set myself, under God's direction, the task of finding out what the Bible really says on the subject of divorce and remarriage.

The Importance of Bible Study

I have studied the Bible for many years under the tutelage of a couple with a useful knowledge of Hebrew and Greek. The husband wrote the following words in my Bible just before they left the district due to their need for social and family care. They now are staying near relatives.

An Elder's Story

Near the end of a long life,
I look back on a walk with the Lord,
started
at the age of 22 and a wonderful marriage of over 60 years
have always sought to
study the Bible accurately,
and thus, have something valid and worthwhile,
to pass on to others.
21/3/17

Cana's Experience

Cana was a member of Elder's Bible study group, until
they moved away recently to a care home. Cana wrote, I
have found Psalm 121 very helpful to me in my life.
Since I have been at this Bible study,
the Old and the New Testaments have come to life. I
have a better understanding of the Jesus there.
I believe the Holy Spirit
is well understood in my life now.
- Cana-

Younger's Experience

Younger is a young member of our Church home group.
ISAIAH54:1-ff
The Lord is my husband.
He is the one who loved me first,
From the start, He was there.
From the foundations, I belonged to Him.
So therefore I love Him unconditionally.
He is all I will ever need and want and desire,
For evermore, I will praise His name.

Ideas about Marriage When You are Young

She sees the movies,
Imagines the feeling,
and wonders what she's missing,
especially when it comes to kissing.
Men think, they *are just like we are,*
But really hope they're not.
So they have their fling,
Experiment,
And then lust hits the ceiling.

CInDys

Abuse should *never* be part of Christian family life

Bitterness
Root out the bitterness through spiritual warfare.

Divorce in its self is a form of abuse.

The word used in the Old Testament is a word for the cutting off or slaughtering of the enemy.

There is no divorce so final, as killing one's spouse;

It is certainly, not loving a wife or husband in a Christ like way. Christ *loved the Church and gave **His** life for her.*

God gives life. Satan devours and terminates it, if he can manage it. He loves to get into marriages and destroy family life in the process.

Love is not selfish or vengeful; it does not seek its own way. It cares more for the other person.

It is not self-serving.

Domestic Abuse
-A True Story-

He tried to control her emotionally, even before they married, but this got worse and turned to physical abuse after they married.

She left him eventually, taking her two girls with her. She stayed with a friend in a very small marital house.

He would come round to wherever she was staying and beg to be taken back, many times.

Eventually she gave in on two occasions, but the whole scenario started again, and so she filed for divorce. She eventually remarried and apparently is much happier now.

This is a prime example of a divorcer against a prospective divorcee. The divorcer is breaking his marriage vows each time he abuses his wife. Abuse is divorce –it is the killing of a relationship.

An abused person needs the Church's help. That help might be to find her a place of refuge, preferably amongst Christian people who can show her Christ's love. We should have nothing to do with people who pretend to be Christians but do not act that way, and so we should give her refuge from her abuser.

The bible teaches us, to judge those in the Church, and tolerate those outside the Church, who do not know any better. They need to find Christ, and they need to see pure, loving lives around them that attract them to Him.

The Church's Responsibility

Leaders are responsible to discern who the divorcer is (aggressor) and who is the injured party when a marriage is breaking down, especially when violence or adultery is the cause. The Church needs to comfort the injured party and discipline the aggressive divorcer with tough love, especially if he or she is seeking a divorce because of an adulterous relationship on the divorcer's part.

Deception

Deception can creep in very cleverly in the latter scenario. Often the unfaithful one will accuse his partner of unfaithfulness in order to get a biblical excuse for divorce.

In the Old Testament, if a fiancé gave his girlfriend a bad name, saying she had been immoral, but she *hadn't*, he was forced to marry her and was not allowed to divorce her for his whole life (Deut. 20:19). This also illustrates to some extent how important the good name of a prospective partner was in biblical times.

It helps us to understand the predicament Joseph was in when he thought Mary had been unfaithful. A daughter of Israel was a special person, part of the pre-Christian Church in a manner of speaking, and a daughter of Israel is meant to marry one of Israel's sons and no one else.

Marriage to an Unbeliever

The apostle Paul told the Church to make sure that couples always marry **"in the Lord"**.

The only exception could be that the possible divorcee was already married to an unbeliever before he or she was converted or 'called'.

In this case, believers were encouraged to pray earnestly for the spouse and children of the marriage, to come to the Lord Jesus.

It is interesting, that children too would come under special prayer support, and thus they would be set apart, prepared for holy living in answer to the Christian spouse's prayer.

Church leaders and friends need to help in this process.

The Divorcer

The Christian divorcer should be treated and considered differently from the victim and would need tough, loving discipline with the aim of getting him (or her) to change the direction of the behaviour and turn back to the "wife of youth, the wife by covenant".

In other words, the first wife is the important one.

These disciplines and prayers are all part of spiritual warfare.

Calling and Ministry

> We need to know our calling and decide what we are dealing with in a ministry situation. We need to find out from the start whether we are dealing with believers or non-believers.
> We need to get our priorities right.
> What are we aiming at?
> Are we looking to win a soul for Christ?
> A person's eternal soul is even more important than his marriage.

God wants us to fight for our relationships. I think that in many cases, just repeating part of God's word over a person will rescue a person. But the whole truth needs constant application, and constant follow-up is essential. This should eventually do the trick.

We should wean them off the easy milk of God's Word and encourage them onto the more difficult strong meat, or challenging doctrines.

We must remember also that Jesus contradicted Satan in this way, with the whole truth of His Father's word. The devil quoted half-truths that seemed to be biblical, but they were a subtle deviation from the *real*, truth and Jesus's reason for coming to earth to die for us.

The Bible is our sword. We need to realize that we are not struggling against flesh and blood, but against princes of darkness who will enter any foot holes they can find. Leaders need to be well equipped to counter the devil's devices.

Marriage Vows

I must emphasize how important these are. The traditional ones are based on many years of experience of what keeps a marriage together; they have stood the test of time. Many of us have promised to stay together with mutual faithfulness as a priority – "for better or for worse, for richer or for poorer, in sickness and in health", to name some of the most important promises.

For my own part, I missed out on "obey" and said "honour", because I thought I wouldn't be able to keep to the obey part and would be telling a lie. This proved to be a problem later on in our marriage of thirty-two years.

In the early days of our marriage, it was a joke for friends.

I think he was quite proud of the fact that I was strong-minded but later on, things changed.

Sarah did call Abraham lord but. I do not think this is necessary today and can get close to idolatry; it it is I think, a false interpretation of submission.

We should lovingly submit to *one another* as believers. This is not only true with husbands, but some of us get near to worshiping pastors, especially if they have a healing gift. Although we serve each other, we should do so without being "a respecter to a person or persons" (James 2:8–9). Jesus is the head of His Church, and leaders in any case, should not lord it over the flock.

David Instone-Brewer throws some interesting light on the misunderstood teachings about submission. He points out, as I understand it, that family submission originates from Greek philosophy more than Jewish. Aristotle had a great deal to do with it, as he considered how to remedy the moral chaos of his time that made a parody of family life. In fact, family life was almost non-existent.

Christians, took over some of this teaching, as the Romans did, and applied it to biblical standards of submission.

We as Christians, however, need to keep in mind that all believers are required to submit to one another in agape love, sharing the good provision that God gave us.

There was no needy person amongst them in the early church, as great grace was on them all. We also should act out this love, which shares with the needy See Ephesians 5:21 and Acts 4:34. Random acts of kindness, when inspired by the Holy Spirit, are very fruitful.

We need to remember, that Jesus will say 'Well done good and faithful servant when we reach the end of our journey. I believe, this will include our faithfulness to our marriage vows.

Chapter 6

Christ in,
My marriage as it begins

Life was difficult, in the early days of our marriage, especially as we were both at college at one stage. We were married while I was training. We did not have a home of our own so we began our married life in a house share.

One of my most embarrassing moments was when I spilled oil over the kitchen floor in our first house share. I remember skidding over it as I tried to clean it up – very unsuccessfully, I might add.

Later, we stayed in an upper room in the home of an older church member. She asked us to leave after about a year because we made too much noise walking to and fro in the room above her. It was her house, so we left.

Next, we shared a house with a woman who was separated, and was getting help from her church for her loneliness. We were also too noisy for her and had to leave after about three years. We shared several houses after this, together with our two girls, who were under five. This meant that we could not have a free, spontaneous relationship and had to try to keep quiet with two small children who were not very good at keeping quiet. Neither were we!

The other day on Christian radio, there was a joke about a man who went up to his wife with a cup of water and two aspirins. She responded, "What's that for? I haven't got a headache?" He laughed and exclaimed, "Gotcha."

I was not given to, "headaches", or avoidance tactics I need to say. These are unfair, I think, and deprive the other of an essential part of marital love.

I had never had another marital partner, through life. I relied on my then husband and various books we shared regarding how to conduct married life.

Most books of course are an interpretation of Bible truth.

We misinterpreted some of the guidance we read about, and I think we chose some books that fitted best what we wanted to believe.

I have come to realize that the overall teaching of the Bible needs to be applied in all aspects of marital love

Christ in, unpleasant truths.

I am trying to cover both sides of the truth here, and that includes the unpleasant truths that most of us do not want to hear. Nobody likes to hear that she is in the wrong but Jesus did not hide these facts from His disciples. He even told Peter, "Get behind me, Satan."

If only we would give one another a fair hearing, or at least bring a witness into situations, especially in the early days of our marriages. We have to work at marriage. We need to learn to understand one another from the start.

Children

Children suffer the most when a marriage breaks down. We need to forgive our parents for their mistakes.

Christ in,
Forgiveness

Are you *sure,* you've forgiven,
or do you tell it around
how badly you were treated
without any grounds?
You were a really good wife;
no one can doubt that.
Forgiving was easy
for him, but not you.
But in all situations,
you must say what is true.
Tell him his fault
is what Jesus said.
If he doesn't receive you,
then bring in a friend.
If you are still not received,
then bring in the Church.
They should be able to find
out the truth.
If he's in some deep sin
and will not repent,
then the Church must decide
that this marriage should end.
You still must forgive him,
though he sues for divorce.
He's an outsider now, no longer your spouse.
Your God will support you, your Father is He.
He'll support and defend you forever; you'll see.
CInDys

Why Does God Hate Divorce?

"Yet you say for what reason?"

Because the Lord has been a witness between you and the wife of your youth, against whom you have dealt treacherously, though she is your companion and your wife by covenant.

But not one has done so who has a remnant of the Spirit. And what did that one do while he was seeking a godly offspring? Take heed then, to your spirit, and let no one deal treacherously against the wife of your youth.

For I hate divorce, says the Lord the God of Israel. "And him who covers his garment with wrong" says the Lord of hosts. "So take heed to your spirit, that you do not deal treacherously." You have wearied the Lord with your words. Yet you say "How have we wearied him?" In that you say "Everyone who does evil is good" in the sight of the Lord and He delights in them, or "Where is the God of justice?" (Mal. 2:14–17)

Children (God's offspring) suffer most when a marriage breaks down.

Christ in, Life's Changes

Physical changes in young people

It does not matter how old young people are. When their bodies start to change, they begin to **think they are ready for a full relationship with the opposite sex.**

But they don't know how to control their feelings, and even schools promote the idea that promiscuity is natural and even desirable. They do this by giving out condoms and encouraging abortions without parental consent in some cases.

I fear for young men and women, who are encouraged to use birth control methods, so early in life, and who are given the impression that being a virgin is not cool. I think it is still true that young men would prefer to marry a virgin, But what has been said to me, is although this is the case, *there are so few virgins about.*

Another important factor is that young women in particular don't realize how precious their virginity is, and that once they have lost it, how vulnerable they are to predatory males.

It is a problem as old as time itself. Many girls love babies and have the nurturing instinct, though they may not realise it.

Jewish women *did* realize this fact and were proud to give their husbands as many children as possible. Many Israeli women, in fact, appeared to value motherhood more than their husband's fidelity, if Sarah's relationship with Abraham in the Old Testament is anything to go by. She gave her husband to Hagar, her servant, and all kinds of disasters were the result.

While I lived abroad, women would become pregnant, on purpose, simply because they did not want to live on their own. Even though the Bible teaches that *marriage* is honourable for all. They made it clear that they had no intention, of marrying the father of their child. They were clearly not considering the child's future, and they overlooked the fact that children need both a mother and a father.

Multiple relationships

A man is told to, cleave to his wife, *not wives,* in the Old Testament. In the New Testament, Paul says, "Husbands, do *not* divorce your wives." The latter is an umbrella statement and therefore, in the plural.

When people came to the Lord in the country in which I worked abroad, we had to deal with multiple relationships and the children born from them. We had to prayerfully help fathers to decide which relationship should be a permanent marital one, and we encouraged them to support (at least with food and produce from the fields) their illegitimate partners and offspring. We believed church members would help as much as they could, but they were all very poor, and it was difficult.

Today's New Believers

Many people believe that there will be a huge influx of new believers, young and old, in the end-time Church, and these will include many one-parent families who will need help for many physical and spiritual issues. Maybe they will not be the same problems as we experienced abroad, but they are serious issues all the same.

As revival breaks out over all the earth, we need to be ready. For this reason, we need to prepare ourselves and be ready to step in and help the children of one-parent families, whatever the reason they are in this condition. They will need mentoring and parenting by two parents, both male and female. For this reason, Church-based marriage or remarriage should be encouraged. God loves the children and wants them to have a complete family life.

The Church family needs to teach and exemplify pure and holy living standards. Children need to be taught to cherish their virginity and save themselves for their prospective husbands or wives. In other words, where children are still virgins, they should be encouraged to stay that way until they meet the man or woman God chose for them. They may need help to find the right person, but God found Isaac the perfect mate to marry and used a servant to point him in the right direction; this was a woman who was kind to both the man and his beast.

Shakespeare made the comment in a play, "Kindness in women, and not their beauteous looks, shall win my heart." We all need kind hearts of Christian agape love if we are going to measure up to 1 Corinthians 13's standards and make our marriages and other relationships work.

Love Is Courageous for the Truth

Virginity is precious, and young people need teaching this fact. They need to stay pure for their prospective marriage partners. This kind of love is a wonderful thing, and should not be downgraded by wrong teaching in schools, or anywhere else.

It's true that we are made pure through the blood of Jesus, shed to wash away our sins. Thus, we are being made pure as virgins again, but like with David, the results of sin don't always disappear. We might still have illegitimate children to bring up.

God might lead us to a faithful marriage partner after conversion (if we are biblically divorced.). By God's grace, even the children from the previous marriage might be catered for, if the second marriage is a godly one. But while in the world, we all need the strength of the Holy Spirit in order to live in integrity, faithful to our marriage and to our Christian partners.

Boundaries

I think that in the case of our marriage and family life, we were overstretched and overcrowded with other people's problems while we tried to serve God, as part of our family life. This exacerbated our own family difficulties. Sharing our home with other troubled people simply did not work.

More than anything, we needed the local church to be behind both of us, particularly in prayer. We needed them to pray for us, and our marriage, rather than stand aloof and criticize, as some did. As you can imagine, the gossip went to town while we were trying to do this work, and we also received hate mail, which was devastating to me.

Mutual forgiveness, however, is the only answer to all these events. They all, came to pass, as Jesus said in an old version of the Bible, and I continue to pray for those inadvertently injured by our work and eventual marriage breakdown.

One man rang us up recently and told the whole family, one by one, how we had helped him through our work. He said he would not be here now if we had not helped him and shared our home with him He told us, he was now a married man and is involved in church life. He rang up again recently to tell us of a failed operation that nearly cost him his life. We renewed our prayers for him.

Christ in, Dreams

As we look back on Joseph's dreams in the Old Testament, his family clearly understood what the bowing of the wheat, sun, moon, and twelve stars was all about. The bowing and the quantity of symbolic items had clear significance. In the past, we also had words of knowledge from church members, but somehow they were not used as guidelines at the time. I pray now that similar works to ours will learn from our mistakes, and all concerned will pray and overcome the temptation to quit the work or the marriages that are deeply involved in mentoring the work of reconciliation. We need a united body of believers – this is the only long, narrow road to victory.

A Dream on 27/02/14

I have dreamed many times that I was taking a journey in the mountains, always by foot. Two men were accompanying me, one on the left and the other on the right. They got distracted, and one of them started to talk with a woman sitting near one of the rickety huts by the side of the road.

I was concerned because in the past, I had found myself travelling alone in the dark, and I was therefore, forced to stay in a hut with strangers. I was afraid, in these previous dreams and was not at all sure I was safe. I waited for the man to finish talking, and we continued our journey. I tried not to say anything about the delay.

After this, one of the two decided he wanted to rest, and he did so. By this time, I was very concerned and recounted the times darkness had fallen in my journeys, and I had been forced to stay the whole night with total strangers. I pleaded with them to wake up and restart the journey, or I would have to travel on my own.

This recurring dream has made me think again of the journey of life and John Bunyan's Pilgrim's Progress, which was such a help to me in my early teens when I was first converted and born again into Jesus's kingdom life.

John Bunyan used his time in prison describing the life of a true Christian as a journey to the Celestial City. He met various characters on the way, and some helped him on his way, whereas others led him astray. I know we do not fight against flesh and blood according to Apostle Paul, but we fight the fight of faith in order to overcome rulers of darkness with light.

Christian's true friends are Faithful and Hopeful.

We see Christ in the hero Christian. May He also be seen in our lives.

Sexual abstinence
(Exodus 21:10ff)
Support the estranged wife.
Let her go without any financial bribes
(1 Cor. 7:5ff)
If there is a mutual decision to separate for a while, perhaps for prayer-
keep it brief,
make sure you are agreed about it,
in order to avoid temptation.

Apostle Paul managed to *stay single* and pure, and so can we.

Your questions
and answers.

What have you learnt from the Bible and other reading, that has changed your mind about what truth really is?

_____

_____

_____

_____

_____

Christ in,
The spoken language

It seems to me that for most of us, our native language and background, and even theological study, can hinder us, through preconceived ideas, from finding out what the Bible really says about certain issues.

The most difficult issue that I have tried to read about and discuss with friends and family, is the one I am tackling now; that of Christian remarriage after divorce, and how to prevent divorce in the first place.

Christ in, our understanding of the Bible.

The Bible is clear on the subjects discussed here

It is our understanding of biblical backgrounds and thought forms that are at fault. Most people will not *even think* about the subject of divorce in the church prayerfully, but they simply consider that a divorce must have been "six of one and half a dozen of another", and we should not ***judge.*** We need to ask ourselves what judging is, from a complete biblical point of view. In other parts of the bible, the Lord instructs us to make "righteous judgements".

If we are genuine Christians, our sins have been born in Christ's body on Calvary.

> He died that we, might be forgiven.
> He died to make us good.
> That we might go at last to heaven;
> *Saved, by His precious blood.*

This old hymn reminds us that we *are,* forgiven and that if we judge ourselves through repentance, we will *not,* be judged. Our sins are covered and forgiven. The time will come when we shall judge angels with His righteous judgements.

Paul said we *should* judge sin in the Church; otherwise, the whole Church will be, contaminated by its growth amongst members.

If we do not bring discipline to immoral situations, we will come under God's condemnation, and the light that is the Church is in danger of being, put out.

The Church in Revelation was severely condemned for condoning the sinful behaviour of Jezebel, who was polluting God's people with her loose ways. She, like Jezebel in the Old Testament, was to be thrown out, in no uncertain terms together with her sin-soaked lovers were to be thrown out with her. It is the non-repentant, lustful sinners who need discipline, not the ones like Joseph, who get slandered for escaping the advances of the temptress who was his boss's wife. However, if a divorcee yields to the temptation of getting his or her own back, and if the divorcee commits adultery or fornication as a retaliatory act, or even as an act of self-comfort after divorce has already taken place, then that person also becomes a divorcer, and under the law of disobedience, he or she needs to repent. That means doing the opposite of this behaviour and asking for the Creator's empowerment. Even Jezebel was given time to repent, but obviously she refused to do so and was condemned because of this.

How could, Jezebel, and her lovers, be allowed to remarry. Like Saul of old, they had permanently hardened their hearts. Until God took over and hardened all their hearts for them, *they could* no longer repent. Today's Jezebels could easily get an incurable sickness. In fact, I think God is calling out through her experience. He is pointing out the dangers of promiscuity not only to the individual but also to future generations. Most people can see that children imitate their parents' behaviour, and so marriage becomes less common. This is why so many couples today cohabit, saying that the marriage contract is just a bit of paper. This is not being modern.It is a syndrome that is as old as the hills. The marriage contract was legalised in the first place to protect the woman and her children. If a man does not need to make this commitment, he will be even more likely to wander off to new pastures, more convenient relationships.

Couples are talking today about short-term marriage contracts of two years duration. What will this do to the stability of family life? As believers, we must learn to bring unselfish, long-term commitment back into our marriages. The Lord Jesus cared for women and opposed divorce.

- In those days, it was usually men who were the divorcers-

"Liberated" women today, may be worse than men in this respect; putting their careers before the welfare of their families.

Women's rights

In Jesus's day
Women had few rights outside marriage.

Even in Moses day, witnesses had to sign a divorce document, but their main task was to encourage the couple ***to stay together***. This factor is important, because there is documentation to show that men tried to divorce their wives for things like burning the dinner or raising their voice in public. You can see why Jesus pointed out that Moses only allowed divorce because men had hard hearts and wanted to be free to cherry-pick their partners as the mood suited them. Jesus made it quite clear that His Father and our Creator, God, had not intended divorce in the first place. Man would leave his father and mother and cleave unto his wife; they would be one flesh. Divorce would tear them in two and desecrate their family life. Multiple divorces would be extremely messy affairs, leaving bleeding emotions everywhere. It is no wonder God hates it.

It wasn't only men who did the divorcing. Jesus told the woman at the well that she had had several husbands, and the man she was living with was not her husband. She was amazed at this word of knowledge, repented immediately, and became the first woman evangelist.

Also, the woman caught in adultery who was up for stoning clearly repented. All her accusers left when Jesus convinced them of their own sins. The woman stayed with Him until she heard His words of pardon, and I'm sure He empowered her to do so when He told her, "Go your way and sin no more."

Some people seem to think that Jesus condoned prostitution because he went to wedding celebrations and had meals with outcasts such as tax collectors and prostitutes. But, as He said at the time, He came to call sinners to ***repentance,*** not the self-righteous who thought they didn't need to repent. They thought themselves too good to need to repent.

Unfortunately, it will be too late to repent once they face the gaping gates **of Hell**.

In His mercy, however, God gave even the notorious prostitute Jezebel time to **repent,**

While there is ***Life***, and the conscience is still touchable, there is also ***Hope*** through Christ's mercy.

Jesus taught that premeditated remarriage after divorce to a faithful partner was premeditated adultery. My late then husband stated clearly God would forgive him because He is merciful. I'm sure this is true, but it does not alter the fact that his divorce could have been premeditated, disobedience. There is a difference between a one-off, impulsive sin that is repented of, by honest confession, and perhaps the couple moving away from the source of the temptation (even to the extent of moving house). This is perhaps, the sort of change, Jesus meant, when he said it was better to cut a part of your body off than to sin rebelliously with that part. Paul taught young Christians that if their spouses had left them, possibly because they were pagans and did not want to be associated with a Christian partner, then they should let them go. Slaves should also accept freedom if possible. If a Christian is married to a pagan or any kind of unbeliever, such as a New Age person, this is a kind of slavery too. Scripture needs to be rightly divided, however Jesus's intimate friends asked him what he meant when they were alone with him in the house. On first hearing, they clearly thought that Jesus was teaching it was better not to marry at all, if it was such a difficult relationship. Perhaps they thought it would be too difficult to get free from an unsuccessful marriage, if divorce and remarriage were adulterous. Jesus then pointed out to them during this time in the house that some people have the gift of celibacy, and some don't. Marriage is a way of life, and the married person is obligated to consider the needs of his or her partner, and of course the children of that marriage. "One man, one wife, one love through life", as the old song goes, is certainly a good ideal and a biblical concept.

Men and women today are now talking about temporary legal marriages. These are exactly what the Bible rules out. The "one flesh" of marriage is torn apart again and again, and children are thrown into utter confusion. It's not possible to hide these affairs from other people's children. Bad news spreads like wildfire, corrupting morals everywhere.

Christians should never allow themselves to be dragged into this quagmire of infidelity. Who of us cannot honestly admit that we would love a faithful relationship that would last till death parts us? We should pray, "Forgive us our divorces, and for condoning divorce by our careless attitudes."

How can we, as believers who will have to give an account for every idle word we speak while living on this planet, excuse ourselves of vows made before the living God, whether they're made in a registry office or a church building? We the people are the Church, and our bodies are temples of the Holy Spirit.

We often forget that repentance does not mean just having a good cry, feeling sorry for a short time, and then doing the same thing again at the next opportunity. It's turning around full circle and facing in the opposite direction, or beginning to do the opposite of what was done before. If converted, we should be well on the way to breaking our old bad habits. We have the Spirit of God to empower us. I am sure you'd agree that if Apostle Paul heard Christ speak to him on the road to Damascus, telling him the danger of kicking against hard objects and that he was kicking against Christ as he killed Christians; had he continued killing Christians in spite of his vision, we would have doubted the authenticity of his conversion.

We are not *saved by* good works, but we're certainly *saved for* them.

There must be a change of our way of living that is clear to those around us.

The way we live at home and work is vital. It may be a struggle, but we need to become more like Jesus. Jesus loves us the way we are, but He loves us too much to leave us that way. There is no sinner too bad to repent and have his life turned around through the power of the Holy Spirit.

Taming the Tongue

The first thing that needs taming in most of us is the tongue. How many marriages end in the divorce court because of a nagging or complaining tongue? This discord is often about money. It's how money is spent by the other partner, that causes so many rows. "Freely you have received, freely spend" seems to be the main motto today, if the piles of food in supermarket trolleys are anything to go by. You would never think we were on the brink of a recession.

Instead of sitting down together, making a joint budget each week, and giving one another a cash allowance for essentials and maybe a small amount of pocket money – *and sticking to it* – couples give into the adverts and spend money like water. Then arguments and quarrels break out once debts piles up. Divorce can be the end result. Marriage is a partnership and needs to follow the rules of the game.

James points out that even the violence of war begins with a loose and uncontrolled tongue.

>We will have to pay the penalty for every word we say.
>The light will show the poison and the covered-up decay.
>Our words are very powerful, and destroy they may.
>So hold your tongue,
>Give it a rest.
>Give to God your best.

>ClinDys

A person who can control his tongue, is greater than a person who controls an army, we read in Proverbs.

Perhaps, some wars over the earth begin with violent tongues; by people who speak before they think; Revenge is in the air, and so they follow that spirit on its road to disaster.

Christian marriages can follow this road too, in spite of Jesus' teaching about turning the other cheek. If Christian families fail in this way, how can we expect, the wars between nations to be, eliminated. Is it because of this fact that Jesus told us wars would continue to the end, and parents and people of our own households would be at one another's throats. In a sense, He brought this into the world, because he foresaw that families would rise up against one another for sectarian reasons, as they did against Him.

We need His pin pointers to right levels of authority in the home in order to overcome discord and even violence in our homes. This is surely, what Jesus meant when He said His presence upon earth would bring a sword amongst nations, and rejection by family members.

This is happening all the time today for Muslims who become Christians but it should not happen through genuine Christian families. We must get back to our founder, who is Jesus the Christ, the Son of the living God, who makes a way when there is no way. Strict adherence to the norms of scripture is the only way to overcome the violence of violent divorce.

Our present culture has swung away from belief in the husband's authority in the home. If a man is not ready to take the lead in family life, then I suggest he is not marriageable yet. On the other hand, if the woman does not respect her future husband enough to encourage him to lead, then this relationship needs to mature. Some churches give Bible-based pre-marital counselling, which is an excellent idea if handled sensitively.

Christian couples are heirs together of all kinds of riches through the gift of grace.

We come to the Father through Grace, and we live by it too. The Bible is very clear about leadership in the Church and in the home. Submission, however, does not mean the church member or wife, should relinquish all authority and give up individuality or the ability to make decisions. It is simply that someone has to make the final decision in the home. Biblically, this needs to be the husband.

Chapter 7

Violence in Society

I am increasingly convinced that the days of increased Violence Jesus warned us about, are on our doorstep.

There are crises upon crises through- out the world.

They show no sign of abating, and although Christians are doing their best to assist the victims of each struggle, and some countries are opening their doors to refugees- the Lord showed me this would happen, when I first began writing this-

There are signs that violence is to be part of the refugees experience where-ever they go.

There have been four notable incidents here, during the last two weeks. Only yesterday, there was one near where I am writing this, and today, two people were killed and many were wounded through a nail bomb attack in a crowded city area.

As I study the scriptures, I am increasingly convinced that we are in the final, end times, before Jesus returns, because violence is beginning to fill the earth.

God's merciful judgement must begin in the house of God, His Church.

Hidden Sins of Leaders

The hidden sins of many Christian leaders have been exposed during recent years too, and it is often difficult to know if such offenders were really Christians in the first place.

The Bible teaches in Matthew 7:16, that followers of Jesus will be known by their "good fruit", which includes patience

– the opposite of violence and lust-.

When *unrepentant* sin is the fruit of leadership, the question needs to be asked, Is this person really a Christian, or is he or she is an imposter?

Perhaps he or she is a Christian spiritualist, as they sometimes call themselves in their attempts to deceive even the elected bride Christ, the Church (2,Tim. 3:1).

We need honest, self-effacing leadership in order to avoid the pitfalls of modern deceptions. The leader needs to lead in presentation of a clear understanding of both sides of the coin of truth, not merely the part we like that makes us soft on confrontation of what the Bible calls evil. Divorce is an evil that needs clear understanding and discipline in order to eradicate the root of bitterness that caused it in the first place.

I believe it is clear in scripture that honest, Bible-based Church leaders are the ones to discern who is a rebellious divorcer and who is a victim or repentant divorcee. Only the latter may biblically remarry. They are like the repentant virgins or now self-controlled widows whom Paul said it was advisable that they should marry again, rather than go from house to house gossiping and causing trouble, as some younger widows were evidently doing. The New Testament Church was to support the ones who had no other means of support.

Older, chaste, or self-controlled widows who were over sixty years old with no family to support them; widows; and divorcees – not prostitutes or women who had not repented of bad behaviour – were certainly to be supported- It seems

This is an application of the Old Testament teaching, where widows and divorcees were encouraged to return to the priestly family and be given the consecrated food to eat.

In a similar way, the virgin bride of Christ may do the same, eating physical and spiritual food offered by spiritual leaders such as Stephen in the book of Acts. Stephen was a man full of grace, acting as Jesus did at the point of people's needs.

He was one of the men, who served at tables. He did this to help the widows with their physical needs of food.

If the widows were found to be divorcers, as Jezebel was, I'm sure they were crossed off the register.

Also had the prostitute whom Jesus forgave and empowered to go away and sin no more; had she continued in prostitution, she would *not* have been included on the widows register either.

Division

Division in the Church is caused by sin of the divisive person, not by the person sinned against.

As I have pointed out before, I have called the divisive person the divorcer here, because English lacks a concise word to describe this person.

Chapter 8

The Divorcer versus the Divorcee

Discipline

Disciplining the divisive person may help to stop the landslide of broken relationships that are sure to follow an acrimonious divorce.

When a man is under discipline and challenged in a biblical, way, He may be encouraged to repent and go back to the wife of his youth, his wife by covenant. This happened in one case I know of. One of the elders challenged the offender, and after discipline, he returned to his wife and apparently, was helped to reconcile with her.

Discipline of the Domestic Abuser

Violence is a destructive and dangerous demon, and the victim will need careful protection. As pointed out before, the person controlled by this is usually the divorcer, and he is often the aggressor in a marriage breakup.

The act of divorce in itself is also a type of violence to what should be a lifelong loving and giving relationship.

In the beginning, God did not intend for it. A man should leave his father and mother and cleave to his wife (not wives). Men took on various wives in the Old Testament, according to their natural tendency. This usually led to trouble. This wasn't God's best by any means.

They may have divorced one after the other in some cases, or supported a harem of wives like Solomon. Jesus pointed out however, that this was adulterous behaviour or bigamous behaviour, and it was not His best plan for families.

Multiple relationships hold many hazards. Solomon's heathen wives led him into idolatry, which may happen to God's people today if they marry non-believers.

Our Christian call should be our priority throughout life.

Single people who have multiple intimate relationships are equally culpable. The Bible says this is fornication and is physically harmful.

Others outside marriages may be guilty too; they may be encouraging promiscuity by forbidding or discouraging true Church-blessed marriage between a man and a woman, at least by their example.

Signs of Infidelity

His eyes light up when he sees her.
She returns his glance, so coy.
It reminds her of when she was single
and admired by a neighbour's boy.
It doesn't matter he's married;
it makes it so much more fun,
especially when she is noticed
by his youngest unmarried son.
Like Joseph,
He should run.

CInDys

Who is free to remarry?

I have come to believe that sincere divorcees who are not sinning sexually are termed unmarried in the Bible, are grouped alongside widows in the New Testament, and are free to remarry (1 Tim. 4:20).

The problem today is probably the same as it was in Moses' day and is a reason why he gave divorce laws in the first place which many lawmakers have tried to follow in the past.

Christ in,
Faithfulness to one wife

There has always been the need for husbands to be the husband of "but one wife" (1Tim. 3:12), *not wives.*

The main difference between a Christion and a fake believer, is that the Christian will deeply regret that he has let Jesus down, whereas the hypocrite will only be sorry that he has been found out and will repeat his sin at the next opportunity.

We are told to beware "wolves in sheep's clothing" (John 10:12). Both Jesus and Paul warned these would enter the flock by "some other way".

The imagery is of a divisive person secretly devouring the flock. -One who drives his wife away through violence- could fit this category-. He has the hidden intention of devouring her even though she is part flock for whom Christ died. He certainly does not love her as Jesus did. Christ loved the Church and gave up His personal desires, for her benefit. We all have to display fruits of repentance (Matt. 7:17) and love, especially towards our husbands or wives.

Jesus is our helper in building peaceful relationships.

Distinctions between a Divorcer and a Divorcee

I have come to believe that throughout scripture, and especially looking at interpretations from Hebrew and Greek, the Holy Spirit makes it clear that there is an important distinction between a divorcer and a genuine divorcee (the often unwillingly deserted spouse). In the Old Testament, she, together with widows, is the only one allowed back into the priestly family.

I have also come to believe that amongst the widows cared for by Steven, there would have been divorcees. The Bible does not refer to former prostitutes as we might, for example, although some of them certainly became Christians.

In the times of Paul, at least, a polite name for those deserted by their heathen husbands would probably have been widows. Even Jezebel, a well-known prostitute, tried to forget the "shame of her widowhood" by deception and pretending that she had married (Rev. 18:7).

The Church was, severely reprimanded, for condoning her lustful behaviour.

In a similar way, Church leaders today need to rescue spouses who are married to promiscuous people, ministering to practical needs as the early Church seemed to do.

The Widow's Register

The register was a list women who were all alone and especially when they were past the age of sixty. (1 Tim. 5:3).

Jesus responds.

Jesus often had to answer questions from hypocrites, who were perhaps looking for an excuse to divorce their wives and marry someone, whom they may already have had their eye on.

The disciples discussed these teachings with Jesus, indoors later.

They obviously did not think that Jesus was saying divorce was feasible as a second chance, if a man had an ulterior motive in view that involved disposing of the faithful wife "of his youth, his wife by covenant" (Mal. 2; Matt. 19:1–14). Jesus was speaking to people who were already committing heart adultery.

Possibly, there were violent husbands in the crowd who were nurturing hatred in their hearts.

These should not remarry and spread the rot.

God's Widows

I do not believe that the deserted spouse was even included in His teaching. Had she lived in Old Testament times, she would have been made a widow, as adultery held the death penalty.

God Himself would be her husband. And, if according to His plan, He would "give her to another" if and when the time was right (Jer. 8:10).

This was especially true for younger widows. They were encouraged to re marry. Perhaps this was so the Church did not get a bad name, and because of the doubtful behaviour of some of these women, such as Jezebel. Married, they would not be accused of having had children out of wedlock.

Older widows came under a slightly different category, perhaps because they were more reliable in their Christian behaviour.

(1 Tim. 5:3–16).They could be more responsible to care for the Church through the work of prayer. Therefore, the Church needed to care for these widows in a special way, perhaps to give them more time to pray. Such widows would no doubt have prayed earnestly for the younger widows and families in the churches.

Family Unity

When there is a precious jewel, there are always numerous imitations. Where there is a marriage made in heaven, there are also many, hypocritical unions based only on personal pleasure. The former are based on the truth of God's Word; the rest are usually destined for disaster.

How, then, can church leaders help couples sort their problems out, and preferably from the beginning?

Spiritual Parents Mentors

The church has the serious responsibility of helping couples both before and after marriage; in a sense, if a couple has been married in the church, they should be divorced in the church, if divorce becomes inevitable. Church leaders need to do all they can to heal the situation when a marriage flounders.

If it was impossible, to do this, it's the church's job to pronounce a marriage irretrievably broken down.

According to Paul, we should not need to go to pagan law courts about church matters, and certainly, it should not be necessary to wrangle and fight before non-believing lawyers or magistrates. This brings division and ridicule to the name of the one we seek to serve. "God calls us to peace" (1 Cor. 7:15).

It is true that the Lord disciplines us all at times, but he often uses godly leaders to pass on His message. He used a man to show David how bad his sin was against his loyal servant Uriah. However, because of David's longing to obey God, he repented instantaneously and with all his heart, when he realized what he had done. Psalm 51 was the result; a wonderful prayer of repentance.

There must be mentors in our churches who are not afraid to speak biblical truth on a personal level, even though the truth hurts all concerned. Mentors need to be aiming for exemplary marriages themselves and not be afraid to let us see their love in action. Exemplary does not mean perfect.

Youth Leaders

Our youth leader was brutally honest about his marital mistakes and got us to be sure we would only marry believers, which was difficult. Only a handful of couples who married from that youth group split up in later life, but unfortunately, I was one of them.

I was naïve, although the Lord warned me in a dream before my marriage took place that the marriage would become like waiting on a cold, desolate platform for a train that would never arrive. Even so, I went ahead and married.

I felt uneasy about many aspects of our relationship but I tend to think now, that I was trying to fulfil my girlish dreams of married love. I had dreams of having, two boys and two girls. I prayed and I prayed for these. God answered *this* prayer.

I chose to ignore the various warnings from relatives who knew us both well and who, for various reasons, thought our marriage would be a disaster.

The Bible teaches us to listen to parents' advice because it may "go well with us", but we seldom do. "Honour your father and mother" (Matt. 19:19) that it may go well with you, and you may live long on the earth

He was my first love, and in spite of these warnings, it did not even occur to me that he might leave me later in life.

I can say now after my experiences, we all need to take the Bible's teachings on the way to success in marriage very seriously. We should listen to our Christian parents and mentors along the way.

The thing about marriage is that it runs along a dual carriageway, and two people have to share the car they drive in, most of the time. I always knew I shared some of the blame for any dissention, but I did not want the relationship to end in acrimonious divorce.

It may not have done so, had there not been another woman involved. (This was the opinion of a relative by marriage who knew the people involved.)

As I said before, we *both* had to want the relationship to work. It takes two determined people to make a lifetime relationship work. If we go through rocky times, we need to tell the full truth to any counsellor who is trying to help us. I think this kind of resolve is essential in all relationships. We need to speak the truth in love at all times throughout the relationship. Sadly, this did not happen in our case.

Leaders need to discern who is telling the truth and who is not, when there are contradictions. It is the truth that sets us free at all times, and it is Jesus' word applied faithfully that makes this possible.

Unfortunately, our counsellor did not discern the truth when speaking to us. He got nearer the truth when his wife was present, but in the end, he gave my then husband an excuse to leave me.

All these recollections are painful, and I want to forget them, but as I have said throughout this work, any bitter roots must be pulled out of my own thought system too. I still have to face up to the truth, as we all have to. Jesus did not ask us to hide our heads in the sand.

One councillor.....Neither should we dwell on the past, but have every thought in subjection to the move of the Holy Spirit.

The Holy Spirit works towards healing in our lives and seeks to help us find deep unity, especially in marriage.

More true stories and a solution.

Cindy's husband was emotionally abusive even before they married.

Eventually, she was forced to leave him, and sue for divorce, because he threatened her life.

There was no doubt that he was the aggressor or divorcer in the relationship.

Her solution was to marry a man who was kind to her, and helped her with her girls, and she helped him with his children.

The couple gives mutual help to one another now, as far as possible with their previous families' cooperation. Although, my friend, has to share custody of her girls, and this is difficult, however, God helps her, as she trusts Him to do so. The main problem now is to introduce any kind of Christian influence to either family, or to encourage them to be interested in having a Christian marriage in the future.

I have also been told of a friend's unmarried brother who has a woman partner who abuses him, and he has almost ended up in hospital more than once. The trouble here is a dependency on drugs, but also the soul tie that keeps on taking him back to his violent and abusive partner. The sister who asked for prayer for her brother has no solution apart from prayer, which we continue to do. We need a miracle of deliverance from this stronghold that overshadows so many lives today. I spoke to her yesterday, and she tells me now that God is answering our prayers for her brother.

Soul ties

Many people, even Christians, do not realize that sexual activity of any kind creates a soul tie that only Christ and His word can break. When Jesus confronted Satan in the wilderness after his mammoth fast, He used the word of his Father God to combat the half-truths that our enemy was feeding Him. It is significant that angels came to minister to Him at that point, and they will do the same for us if we pray and cast out fear.

Prayer and Hinduism

We went out for a meal today, and one member of the group, an Indian lady, told us about her experience of being married to a Hindu man. She did not realize until after the celebration that the ceremony also meant that she had taken on the Hindu religion. They have two older children now, and she has never, been allowed to take them to a Christian Church.

We all prayed for her quietly around the table that day, and I continue to do so.

She had tried on many occasions to let him go, but he did not want to leave this convenient relationship, and so she has not been able to do so. The relationship is financially convenient for him. As far as I know, nothing has worked so far. I continue to pray. It was quite funny to see that the restaurant suddenly emptied while we were praying ever so quietly, and the staff who were attending us, were anxious for us to leave. I felt the Lord was saying to her to keep quiet at home and avoid riling him up, especially about money matters, because he was sure to go round in circles on this issue. I would like her to read the scriptures quoted here that have helped many people through the fire of testing.

I have been asking the Lord for solutions to the problems that marriages face, especially when a believer is married to an unbeliever. There are several couples in such a situation as this, couples who I know personally.

One weekend I met two women, who had marital difficulties that they haven't as yet managed to resolve. In fact, they were not aware of how to tackle their problems in a biblical way. I have therefore been trying to find a Christian person married to a non-Christian who has been seeking to apply scripture to her marriage successfully.

A Rocky Marriage before Conversion

Another friend and her husband became believers about ten years after their marriage. Their marriage went through some rocky times, and they came near to divorce.

Once they became believers, however, things began to change. The husband in particular tried to apply scripture to their situation, and their relationship began to improve. What caught the husband's attention were the words "Husbands, do not divorce your wives".

They are still married today many years later, and what I notice most about them is their kindness to one another and to those who need help or mentoring.

Another friend who has a non-believing husband has felt it necessary to submit to her husband's unreasonable demands, which in her case appears to have become a kind of slavery.

It is a good thing to respect ourselves as well as our partners. Others tend to treat us in the way we expect them to.

Jesus lifted the position of women in the male-dominated society of his time. We need to be balanced today and submit to one another in Christian love (Eph. 5:21).

Our prayer on my friend's behalf is that she win her husband for Christ by her good behaviour, but this should not involve being a door mat for him to walk over.

He needs the Holy Spirit in order to love his wife as Christ loves the Church and gave Himself for it. An overly submissive wife can open herself to abuse, and so we continue pray. We are still doing this,

Chapter 9

Christ in, Disasters.

We are now on the brink of a new millennium.
Every day, we hear of increased violence in so many parts of the world.
There are floods and natural disasters all over the globe.
Surely Apocalyptic prophesies are being fulfilled
before our very eyes.
Revelation
chapter 8: v 1ff.
15/12/99

We Live in Troubled Times

God gives men the gift of discovery.
But in many fields of research,
men and women have twisted
His natural laws
and brought about the possibility
of global disaster and destruction
as never seen before.
And if this is not enough,
they have shaken their fists in His face
because of the results.

Nuclear disasters are predicted
by many people, including a news
paper
that stated boldly many years ago
that one in particular would happen
"if computers are not immediately updated".

This was only one of the unending, destructive results
that affect families worldwide and future generations.
Jesus told us wars and rumours of wars
would accelerate towards the end of time.
We must trust Him
that He is in control,
and not be afraid.

We must watch and pray,
because we don't know the exact time
the bridegroom will come to take us home.
We must be ready!

The Root of Natural Disaster

The root cause of natural disaster can usually be put down
to man's bias towards, selfishness, greed and sloth.
(Prov. 40:1).

Political, Social,and Spiritual disasters, are
usually started by a small spark.

Large disasters are often the result of violent, unrepentant
divisions in Christian homes and churches.
(James 4:1–3).

Divorce must be the epitome of destroyed relationships.

Again and again, Father God describes Israel of the Old
Covenant as a wife who has prostituted herself after idols.

Hosea has to go through the painful experience of being married to a former prostitute in order to show us how God agonizes and suffers terribly at the trauma and terrible discipline He is forced to exact against His rebellious people (Hosea 2:1–2).

But Malachi points out how Father God is ready and waiting to heal the wounds he has allowed (Mal. 2:11–15; Mal. 4:1–6).

The Dark Depths Try to Hide Them

As for ages trees have stood,
Others look so beautiful,
Covered there with bloom.
But with bitter roots surrounding,
The trees will surely die
And soon be bare and prickly,
Spreading hate and gloom,
Then dying.
So pull them out so quickly.
Yes, pull them out today.
Dig deep into the poisoned soil
With Holy Spirit oil.
God's pruning,
God's pruning is painful,
At least for the tree.
It touches on anguish
In you and in me,
Those sensitive places.
In shame we would hide,
Where Satan has prodded
And unto us lied.
He told us that no one would know what we said
When we muttered the words,
"I wish you were dead."
Satan's a liar;
He was from the start
A despicable liar,
A god with no heart.
Resist him today.
Don't let him win.
With Christ in your heart,
You *will* overcome sin.
C in Dys

Chapter 10

**Questions Arising from Personal Experience:
The Divorcer versus the Divorcee in the Church**

Moses made divorce rules, and the leaders in Jesus's time pointed this out. Surely, however, divorce should *not* be an easy process. Why do even experienced people in the Church classify all divorced people together as a mutual disaster area needing identical ministry? Why do they not even question who is right or wrong in the divorce?

In Malachi 3, God appears to empathise with the faithful divorcee.

It's clear that Israel so often acted as a wayward spouse lusting after idols; these were also divorcers.

God also states that He will punish such adulterous divorcers. These remind us of the Pharisees who questioned Jesus for hypocritical reasons about easy divorces.

Jesus is very outspoken in His teaching about divorce to such an extent that some people think Jesus was outlawing almost all divorces in particular, and remarriage after divorce was equally stigmatised in God's sight. Divorce was divorce was divorce, and because God had joined a couple together, not even He would separate them. I don't think this could be the case, however, if it were impossible to do so.

Some people in the Old Testament were told to leave their heathen wives even though they had borne their children and were bilingual.

This does not fit the rest of scripture on the subject, however. Jesus indicated that it was the hypocritical divorcers, who refused to change their ways, who were at fault. He said that if the adulterous divorcer remarried, then he and the person he intended to marry to replace his faithful wife, "his wife by covenant" before God, would be committing premeditated adultery.

In some cases, this might be called bigamy, if they were swinging from one partner to another, as some people do today. Each member of the twosome or threesome would be committing adultery or bigamy in God's sight as long as they as they lived in this way, and they may even risk going to hell with all other unrepentant adulterers (Rev. 2:22).

The apostle Paul states that sexual sin is especially obnoxious and is a sin against one's own body. But it's true that God is very merciful and eternally just. David suffered terribly for his sin with Uriah's wife Bathsheba. He lost her child to what sounded like a cot death. His most handsome son Absalom conspired to usurp his throne, but then he died, ignominiously hanged in a tree when in hot pursuit of David's soldiers. David's throne and reward after his death went to his son Solomon, who eventually lost his godly position through his multitude of wives whose false gods he came to worship.

If we spurn God's mercy indefinitely, there will come a cut-off point. Even the well-known adulteress Jezebel was given a chance to repent, as were Ananias and Sapphira. who lied before the apostles and the Church in general.

It would seem that repentance is nearly always possible for the most ingrained sinners. Even that well-known prostitute Jezebel, was given a chance to repent, but like King Saul in the Old Testament, she hardened her heart and refused to change her lifestyle (Rev. 2:20).

On the other hand, the woman caught in adultery was told to "go her way and sin no more" by Jesus.

He still empowers modern Christians with His mighty resurrection power to stop sinning (1 Tim. 5:7; 1 Pet. 2:24).

I have come to believe, however, that the injured divorcee is encouraged to remarry.

Chapter 11

Christ in, Me and You

My Part in Making a Relationship Work

Forgive, as you have been forgiven

> Forgive your friend.
> Forgive your partner.
> Forgive your husband.
> Forgive your wife.
> Draw a picture of your doing so.

> *Jesus said, "I will only forgive you, if you forgive.*

Write names of people you need to forgive. Then do just that.

_____
_____
_____
_____
_____
_____

Everyone — **who hurts** — **you**

Example:
I forgive you for blaming me.

Our marriage worked in the early days when we kept to our agreement to avoid what we referred to as you-ing. We refused to blame one another and go into history about past clashes. We decided to forgive and forget.

_____
_____
_____
_____
_____
_____

I forgive myself for

_____
_____
_____
_____
_____
_____

Forgive,
Forgive,
Forgive.

Every day,
All the way.
Jesus forgives you all the time you have to forgive others.

My Forgive List.
I forgive you for hating me.

_____
_____
_____
_____
_____
_____
_____

Who May Remarry

In younger widows and divorcees, remarriage is even encouraged, but remarriage for adulterous or violent divorcers is not encouraged. I have come to believe Jesus was saying this is premeditated adultery. Another question is, when is divorce inevitable and even commendable?

Does Jesus's teaching mean that divorce and remarriage is only legitimate for the divorcee who did not break her marriage covenant, or does it include ones who have not given in to pornographic sins, sexual violence, or fornication after the legal divorce? (The Greek *'pornea'.)* which resembles our word *pornography*, means sexual filth (Matt. 19:9).

Is Jesus saying that *any* marriage after divorce would involve them also in adultery, if they married someone else at a later date, I don't think the Bible indicates this at all. Moses did give divorce laws, but he also encouraged married couples to stay together.

It seems to me throughout this study, that God always requires heart repentance and a turning away from any sin at any stage in our lives. If an individual retaliates after a divorce by committing adultery or fornication, God *will* forgive, but there will be sad and difficult results.

Repentance becomes more difficult as time goes by. Our lives need to show that we have repented. Like the soldier in an army, we have made an about turn at the captain's command. We must remember that Jesus often addressed his most tough remarks to hypocrites.

We are hypocrites, if we are looking for an excuse to divorce a faithful spouse and remarry. If this is the case, both partners to the deception are committing adultery, according to Jesus. God hates treacherous divorces if we have this attitude. Like the Pharisees, we are looking for a loophole in order to condone our sinful desires. On the other hand, in view of Jesus's general compassion towards the oppressed and downtrodden amongst people, it is likely that He would support the injured party in a divorce? He would support the real widows or divorcees whose original spouses, according to original laws, would have been stoned, in a similar way to other criminals.

Surely we as the Church, should be disciples too, not hypocritical Pharisees. When His disciples questioned Jesus alone, about the meaning of His words, they **appeared to gain the impression that it would be better not to marry at all in view of Jesus's teaching on the subject.**

**Jesus was saying surely,
that marriage, has always been for life, in God's sight.
If you even *look* at another woman in an adulterous
way, the seed of the act is in your heart.
If you divorce "the faithful wife of your youth" in order to marry
someone else, you and your replacement partner *will also*
Share the guilt of adultery.**

The victim of the adulterous partner does not come into this picture at all, either as a prospective partner for remarriage or one who needs discipline. Other scriptures make his or her position clear.

When we talk about divorce in the Church, therefore, which partner should be brought to task, the divorcee, or the divorcer, or both, as seems to happen in practice, if general attitudes to both parties are anything to go by. At what stage should the Church intervene in order to prevent a divorce that is not inevitable? What should be the aim of all disciplinary practice, these should be enacted hopefully, in an attitude of 'tough love'.

I have tried to answer these questions, over the past five years, and the points that follow also point out the stages, which I have roughly dated, in order to show how I arrived at the following conclusions.

Christ in, Context

We must be able to see Bible truth in its context. What did the people at the time believe God was saying? God's truth does not change one little bit, although the language and culture it's embedded in certainly does.

We need to be sure that we're not interpreting truth according to our preconceived ideas of what God means by certain phrases – what Jesus teaches as a parable, and the teaching behind His healing ministry.

Jesus is our mentor in chief and the main example of what family life should be like in the Church. He is the head of our homes, and we need to act like we're his bride and get rid of the wrinkles of our sin. This attitude of hating sin but loving sinners and forgiving one another from the heart is essential to harmony in the family and Church community.

Family Life

Family life was hugely important in Bible times. We need peace in our families today, but this is not peace at any price. Lists of family relationships seem unending in 1 Chronicles, but they are all with a purpose. Bethlehem was a fairly common first name, for instance, and it became the birthplace of the Saviour of the world. Jerusalem was at one time the city of David; we still know it as "the city of the great King", and we are told by Jesus to pray that peace reigns there.

Blood relationships are crucial according to the Bible.

Nehemiah told the people to fight for their families, their houses, and their land. They fought with swords and spears. We fight with spiritual weapons and our armour intact and in place. We fight the fight of faith, and we have to do this with a united front against the enemy of souls. We live in perilous days because our children are subtly, being drawn into underage sex, pornography, drugs, and alcohol.

<u>May we join the prayer groups, which are getting wonderful answers to prayer today.</u>

<u>And many children are being delivered from drug and alcohol excesses in answer to prayer, especially the united prayer of their parents.</u>

PART 2

Alone Again but marriageable

marriage for life

Anyone who has been divorced from a loved one will realise that the resultant loneliness never leaves completely. The only way the pain of separation can be alleviated, is by making the Lord one's husband.

This wisdom is found in Proverbs 5:18 and Proverbs 7:4–5. In the past, the Lord gave me several verses from the Book of Proverbs on the subject of adultery and the most common **reason for divorce.** This severance means that the "one flesh" of a man and woman is torn apart, and the resultant rejection and sense of isolation from both married and unmarried friends can only be remedied by constantly being alone with Jesus, even in the middle of a crowd. Jesus said that treacherous divorce was akin to adultery.

If we are believers, we are in fact **never alone,** but as our lives and the lives of those around us who judge our situation, must judge along biblical lines. The Church is a body and must act in unison, in agreement with the teachings of scripture. We are told to test the spirits to see if they are from the Lord. A divorce based on deceit *cannot* be biblical.

Dos and Don'ts of Ministry Situations

We must not assume that the person we are ministering to is telling the truth because he or she is an elder or leader in the Church.

Actions speak louder than words in most cases, and if the leader has a tendency to flirt, for instance, especially if married, Jesus taught that first speak to the person alone about it. If he won't accept the word of one person, then take along two or three witnesses. Then if necessary, take it before the Church.

Paul taught in the Bible that we have *a duty* to judge matters of morality in the Church in an honest way, even though the truth hurts all concerned.

In marital situations in particular, it's a mistake to not talk to a couple together.

Talk to both members of couple together, and then with witnesses.

It is especially important that leaders are encouraged to work in a group and not be isolated in a ministry situation. This is especially true though if a man is dealing with a woman with marital problems. It is not wise to discuss marital problems in a one-to-one situation.

Neither should the Church set up a ministry between two people of the opposite sex. Billy Graham often stated publicly that he always travelled around with a male secretary, because he refused to allow Satan to tempt him while he was away from his wife. In one well-known case, prayerful action might have helped prevent some disastrous results that were to follow divorce, which included many copycat and other marital and relational breakdowns in the wake of the divorce.

We need to beware of following King David's sins, but like him, we should repent as soon as we know that we have done wrong. His heart was potentially soft and repentant. He threw himself onto God's mercy. He did *not want* to deceive himself or others when his sin was brought to light. This is what I believe made him a man after God's heart.

His relationship with his arch- enemy's son Jonathan is an advert of true friendship. Jonathan loved David more than his own life. There was no jealousy or lust in the friendship, even under great provocation from Saul, the father.

David mourned Jonathan's death with deep grief, describing Jonathan's love as deeper than a woman's love.

Jesus has given us the best example of this kind of sacrificial love. This should be the basis of our church relationships, and we have the mighty Holy Spirit to empower us in this way. We are not "only human", as some Christians refer to themselves when they slip up. We need to repent as David did and call on Jesus to help us overcome temptation.

David was described as "a man after God's own heart" (1 Sam. 13:14), yet he committed a murderous, adulterous divorce that even non-Christians have heard about today. Perhaps deception crept in, as with some modern, Christians leaders.

These facts have increased my determination to discover biblical teachings about how to avoid such disasters. David should never, be made an excuse for adultery, but rather a reason to avoid it. His heart was broken when he lost Bathsheba's baby. Later, his son Absalom betrayed him – and died a nasty death as a result.

For the rest of David's life, he was a man of war and missed some of the honours of kingship that he would have otherwise gained, had he stayed close to God all his life.

Solomon.

David's son Solomon, was a man who was greatly honoured, and built a greater temple than his father.

Solomon however, became a divorcer, following his father's footsteps as a womaniser.

Sadly, he left it too late to repent and, at the end of his life his many heathen wives lead into idol worship.

I wonder how many broken-hearted women followed in the wake of all the wives in Solomon's harem. In any case, they ended up pulling him into idolatry and ruining his relationship with his Maker.

We must all avoid relationships that lead us into the deception of idolatry and disobedience to the Bible. We must evict lying spirits out of the Church and, if necessary, discipline the people who maybe giving in to deceiving spirits. Actions speak louder than words.

Husbands should only have eyes for their partners by marriage. For instance, a man has admitted to his wife that he intended to replace her with another woman, but he refuses to admit this fact to a counsellor. The divorce process has begun.

Witnesses

Even in Moses's day, witnesses were brought in to dissuade the person from leaving the marriage. This did not happen in the scenario mentioned here. Today, it is all too easy to get a divorce without confronting the divorcee once, and it is a clear example of any cause of divorce from a faithful spouse that the Lord Jesus said would be adulterous, both for the instigator of it and the replacement partner.

Moses encouraged people to judge marriages and, where possible, help them to keep together. Surely today's church leaders should do the same, especially if the couple has been married with the church's blessing. In the above situation, the wife got permission to speak to church elders about the troubled marriage in order to avoid divorce. In the meeting, the main response from the Bible was, "Judge not that you be not judged," and it was "better to marry than to burn". Then they went on to other business.

Prayerful, united action might have helped prevent some disastrous results that were to follow, which included many other marital and relational breakdowns.

What the Bible really says in its completeness is discerned through an understanding of different biblical passages, taken from a variety of reliable versions and being careful not to contradict basic truths on important matters. Even the devil was cunning enough to quote half-truths in an attempt to make Jesus disobey His Father.

The real way to overcome temptation to sin is to be able to understand (and quote if needed) relevant verses based on complete biblical teachings.

My intention here, therefore, is to cut away preconceived ideas, including my own and to call a spade a spade, as the saying goes. It is the recognition of truth in situations that sets us free to do what is right. The Bible is as frank about people's weaknesses as it is their strengths, and I believe that we have to be honest about our own failings and those of others too. "Judge not that you be not judged" could hardly refer to the need to differentiate between right and wrong.

We are not supposed to evade judging what is wrong in another Christian's way of life if we have clear evidence and are sure about what is happening.

Christ in, our future

We all need to look ahead to the future with Jesus's fortitude, and we need to throw ourselves onto His healing mercy. The Lord Jesus will find ways of bringing healing to any rejected member of His Church, but this is usually through the prayer and application of scriptures by God's people (John 10:13).

Divorcees need to resist feelings of being alone again, as well as the actual specific rejections that are usually a factor in the life of any divorcee. These need to be overcome through personal biblical onslaught. Jesus also suffered rejection and the deepest humiliation, and He can help us to defeat our own rejections.

I pray for the grace to forgive. As said before, I would dearly like to help people learn by others' mistakes. The Word says, "Cast all your care on Him for He cares for you" (1 Pet. 5:7). I repeat, rejection is defeated by getting alone with Jesus, who said, "He who comes unto Me, I will in no wise cast out."

New Testament Scriptures

The New Testament makes a clear distinction between the injured party and the initiator of a divorce, by calling the divorcee *apolumenen* in Greek, which could mean one who is unjustifiably, sent away – or a divorcee, as we tend to call both parties. This word is in both Mark 10:12 and Matthew 19:3.

The Divorcer

I have used this word because I have not found a word in English to describe the person who is the aggressor in a divorce action. I believe that much confusion about what divorce really is on both sides of the coin of truth stems from this misunderstanding. English has only one main word to describe two biblical states.

Matthew 5:32 states, "Every one who divorces his wife, except for the cause of immorality, **makes her** commit adultery." The word *porneo* used here covers a multitude of sins of immorality. The following is an explanation of what the New Testament describes as sins worthy of divorce and thus setting the victim free to remarry. Also included is an expression of my insights gained from experience and study.

I could not understand why the woman who had been divorced against her will should be branded as an adulteress, or even a divorcee.

This wording, would make the deserted wife, be even more branded and alone (as she often is), even by Church leaders, who should make a point of finding out who is the adulterous party in a divorce, rather than isolating the partner who is left all alone because her partner did not obey the Word of God on the issue of adultery

(I believe now that **_her_** refers to the **_new_** partner, the one who marries the divorcer. December 2017)

Church Discipline

Proverbs teaches that a person who trusts in God needs rescuing from an adulterous partner (Prov. 2:12, 16–17). To remain with such a one, pretending, that nothing is wrong, would be to condone the next best thing to bigamy.

It is wrong to believe a lie (Rom. 1: 25; 1 John 4:1). There is much unnecessary loneliness amongst deserted and divorced people because other believers are unsure as to which partner is telling the truth when a marriage splits up.

The Church is afraid of taking sides, but the discerning church leader, the Apostle Paul, criticised the Church for going to civil law against one another. He strongly reprimanded them for not having judged a matter themselves, even condoning the actions of a man who was severely sexually immoral. They had, it seems, been sympathetic to the offender, allowing him to have fellowship with them in church. Paul almost demanded that this man be excommunicated or worse, until he repented. He apparently did repent and was received back into fellowship. (1 Cor. 5:4; 2 Cor. 7:8).

The Scandal in Corinth

The church in Corinth took issues of morality seriously after the scandal. His was a church that had only recently come out of heathen occultism, however. We who have known the Ten Commandments for so long, should know better. The sin in the Corinthian Church would have tainted all relationships; this was probably worse to live down than the effects of a modern divorce.

Serious matters, were dealt with by the Corinthian Church, so it could be that in a sense, because couples are married in the Church, they should be divorced in the Church in some cases of adultery –or pornographic sins.-

The Church however, should do all in its power to bring the adulterous persons to repentance (1 Cor. 5:1-2; 2 Cor. 2:7-10). Once the adulterous person has remarried, it is too late to repent and return to the previous spouse, according to Deuteronomy 24:1-4, although in this case in Deuteronomy, the wife was probably the guilty party leading to the split.

Matthew 5:32 has caused many problems for divorcees. I have come to believe that a closer meaning of the words could be that the stigma of the divorce in God's sight will fall at the divorcer's feet. For example, a free translation of the passage could be, "The accusations of having had children out of wedlock, when untrue, will be laid at your feet, divorcers."

This clearly displays why divorce is a stigma, especially for the woman who is bringing up children on her own, in a country where adultery, multiple divorces, and remarriage is rampant. The Church will increasingly need to offer fellowship to the real victims of divorce and not neglect their families. All these need help to make the good master their husband; He alone can heal the pain of a severed vital relationship, especially when it has been caused by divorce. The Lord knows the heart in each situation, but the Church should seek to find out who the guilty initiators of divorce really is so they can be brought to repentance.

Premeditated Adultery

A free translation of Matthew 19:9 is, "Any man who divorces his faithful wife and marries another, commits adultery against his first wife. And so does the woman who marries the unfaithful person."

Who may remarry? Divorce and remarriage is only justifiable for the injured party.

The Old Testament

In the Old Testament, adultery held the death penalty. A wife could have been widowed if her husband sinned against her. Moses's law however, gave a way out, because so many people had "hard hearts" and drove their wives away for trivial reasons.

The word *divorce* is translated in several ways in the Old Testament Hebrew: "caused to leave", "driven off (garish)", "stood away from", "stood off from". Old documents show that women were driven off,

and perhaps turned to other men, for things like: burning the dinner, letting their hair down in public, shouting so the neighbours could hear, or because the husband had his eye on another woman. In those days, women were only able to get support from their families or new partners. Moses tried to regulate matters by making divorce a legal matter. A man had to state to a witness why he was divorcing his wife, verbally and in writing. The witness then had a chance to dissuade the husband in his divorce claim.

It is interesting that, today, the whole divorce can proceed without the husband confronting his first wife once! He can completely absolve himself from responsibility for his wife's future welfare as happened to someone I know. But I can honestly state here that God has looked after her perfectly. There should be no complaints about His support in difficult times.

I am simply trying to find out, from a biblical perspective, how the act of divorce, which is so hateful to God, should be conducted in Christian circles.

Apostle Paul condemns the church for taking up lawsuits before an ungodly court (1 Cor. 6). In the Old Testament, even a wife who had been forced into marriage as a result of slavery was, by Jewish law, to be given food, clothing, and her marital rights. If the man refused to give her any of these, he had to let her go free, without any financial bribe. This was also a kind of legal divorce (Exod. 21:8-11).

Also in the Old Testament, if a man divorced his wife for a trivial reason – for example, he didn't like her anymore – and so she left and married another man, even if her second husband died and the first one wanted her back, he was not allowed to have her (Deut. 24:1-4). The reason given was that "the land would be doubly polluted". Perhaps this means that the mixed parenthood would cause pollution and confusion to the offspring of future generations.

New Testament

It seems that after Matthew's and Mark's renderings of His discourse about divorce, Jesus had reason to say, "Suffer the little children to come unto Me and forbid them not." The selfish and confusing act of divorce profoundly effects children's future. This particular transgression of the fathers tends to fall on their children's shoulders more than any other; they subsequently need the holy Father's love.

In the Old and New Testament

Israel often represents God's people, "the Church" of the Old and New Covenant. We are in part "The new Israel", the branch that has been grafted onto the vine. It seems therefore, priests, may be represented, by faithful Christian leaders, and believers, idolaters are the disobedient ones who refuse God's grace. Christian parents and leaders therefore have a serious responsibility in discernment of moral issues.

A Christian husband has to be truthful, especially if he is seeking a divorce. It was, for instance, a serious matter for a man to lie about a daughter of Israel and give her a bad name. If he said, for instance, that she had slept with another man, and she had not – and she was still living at home with her parents – then the offender was forced by law to marry her and was not allowed to divorce her for the rest of his life. A man also *had* to marry the girl he made pregnant. In both cases, the father could intervene and not allow his daughter to marry the man, exacting a fine instead. Parents had considerable control over their children's behaviour in those days because they were family leaders. Today, there are similar instances in some churches.

I think that in such cases, when there is a church where parents cannot or will not take the initiative, God is the Father should be able to support the poor and ill-used through His Church. It is not a sin to be a victim.

If the victim has not retaliated by committing adultery, then the Church must be careful not to further victimize the afflicted party. I think that according to biblical indications, Church leaders have a duty to find out who is responsible for destroying a marriage.

Hidden hatred and vengeful adultery are often root causes in many cases (James 4:1–7).

If bitterness is the root of the division, then possibly both partners will need to come together and forgive one another, making a fresh start well away from their partners in adultery. Church leadership has a duty to discover, using biblical techniques, which partner is sinning and destroying the marriage through whatever actions. Thus, the Church should lead all parties concerned to repentance, as the Apostle Paul did (1 Cor. 5:3).

Priests

Priests were not allowed, to marry widows, or divorced women, but such women *were* allowed back into the priestly household. This perhaps indicates that certain divorced women were considered victims of circumstance, and were on a par with widows who needed pastoral care.

The priests were to represent the loving Father, who wanted to present his Church as a virgin bride. Such women who had no children were taken back into the priestly family and were encouraged to eat the blessed, consecrated food. The law of love came into operation. Women who were unjustly divorced were not deserted by God or His people; they were not considered outcasts or unclean. They were insiders, not outsiders, in the house of God. Whether, or not they should remarry is not stated, but they were cared for.

A woman, who had been raped or seduced by a boy- friend, was not to be deserted by the boyfriend. Either the parents had to take the victim in, or the culprit *had* to marry the victim.

It is not stated, whether, or not they could remarry.

I doubt that a woman in these circumstances would be encouraged to live with her parents for the rest of her life. Child - bearing, was such an important factor in Israeli life. The New Testament gives pointers about who should remarry and who should not, and the prohibition regarding remarriage that Jesus seems to give is pinpointing cases of adultery. If an individual divorces ***a faithful*** spouse, the divisive spouse *and his new partner will both be committing adultery.*

The inadequacy is in the English language, which uses only one word for both states of divorce. This seems to be where confusion got in.

Leviticus 21:14 and Leviticus 22:13indicates, purity of the priesthood of modern Christian believers is also essential.

We should be/***are*** made pure virgins through the bloodshed of Jesus. How can we continue to follow the ways of the world? Romans 6:1–2 says we need to remain in Him and deeply repent if we soil our Christian robes. Our witness for Jesus should be the reason we live (Rev. 3:4).

We should only have just one wife or husband before God. The two can be "heirs together" of His purity and Grace *both* as one in Him (1 Pet. 3:7; 1 Sam. 15:22–23). God hates divorce, which can bring the one who initiates it into the situation of working against God. I am convinced that God of the Bible is seriously offended by the treacherous and deceitful divorce, which is tantamount to idolatry (Mal. 1:11).

Apostasy

Some marriages are certainly, not made in heaven.

The marriage of Ananias and Sapphira, is a clear example of this fact. A marriage *not founded on* **truth and love towards God**.

A couple who truly love God will also love one another **with *His* love** (1 Cor. 13; Acts 5:1).

In the case of Ananias and Sapphira, surely it would have better for one of them to have divorced when lies first began to creep into their relationship; at least one of them might have been spared that terrible fate (Acts 5:1–11).

Ungodly agreements should never be the fruit of the oneness of marriage. If **the truth,,** is not loved by both sides of a relationship, there is a clear danger of this leading to apostasy or denial of the faith. Divorce might be a preferable option.

In a similar way, the unbelieving or atheist spouse, in the closeness of marriage, can easily lead to the destruction of new-found, faith, unless, the new believer has obedient, full prayer backing.

Both Jesus and Paul advised people to leave relatives or marital partners if it became imperative to do so, and if it was impossible to win them over by good behaviour. The message of the kingdom was clear: they were to win spouses by their lives or "let them go" (1 Cor. 7:15; Matt. 10:37; Matt. 19:29).

When Jesus gave His discourse on the subject of divorce, it must be kept in mind as to whom He was speaking. To begin with, they most likely were hypocrites who were trying to trip Him up in His words and give themselves an excuse to divorce their wives for trivial reasons.

He was saying, "If you divorce your wives for any reason more trivial than their adultery, you will be held responsible for various other adulterous relationships that result from your disobedient act." Hypocrites come into the same category as unbelievers. Jewish believers were not allowed to marry non-Jews, who would often be promiscuous idolaters. Similarly, Christians who marry non-believers may be disobedient to their high calling as part of the bride of Christ (1 Pet. 3).

I have already mentioned one type of divorce that the Apostle Paul refers to in 1 Corinthians 7. Other types of divorce are also inferred **and** may spring up from disobedience. Also, there is a suggestion of a type of marriage separation that may have more chance of reconciliation. Some examples are as follows.

An unbeliever is set to leave his Christian spouse, but the believer is told to try to win him first while he is willing to stay. If at any stage he insists on leaving, she should let him go.

The one who shows more signs of possible marriage reconciliation, however, might be the Christian woman who has separated from her husband, hopefully on a temporary basis. She is told not leave him permanently, but to stay separate or else be reconciled to him. The Christian husband is told not to divorce her. (Possibly today, a woman who suffers from post-natal depression might fall into this category, and the man would need to pray patiently for her recovery.) Paul assumes obedience to marriage vows in Christian husbands, but if the believing husband insists on disobedience to this strong teaching, then he puts himself into a similar category to the unbelieving spouse, who should be allowed to go if he insists on leaving.

"God calls us to peace", not contention and slavery. If we are offered, freedom as Christians, we should take it. God wants us to be obedient slaves of Christ (1 Cor. 7:21). It is our Christian call that is the most important factor in our lives, if we have to choose.

Jesus bought our freedom at a high price, and does not want us to be slaves of men. He said, "Blessed are you when you leave anyone or anything *for My sake and the Gospel*, you will receive a hundred fold in this life and the life to come; with persecutions" (Mark 19:29).

It may be necessary to leave a spouse if it is the only way to support the Gospel of peace and truth, and the results are more freedom to preach it.

Jewish males were told to dismiss their heathen wives when multiple marriages with surrounding tribes had made them lose their Godly, Jewish identity. This could also be the case in some Christian marriages.

Paul may have been one who turned the fact of a wife's leaving into an advantage for the Gospel, giving him more freedom to preach it. He had been a strict Pharisee, a member of the Sanhedrin, where there is some evidence to believe that one of their rules of membership was that members should be married.

Paul referred to himself as unmarried and obviously celibate. Paul told other unmarried readers of his letters who were "like himself" that if they did not have the gift of celibacy like he had, they were not bound but were free to marry their fiancées;

"it was better to marry than to burn with passion" (1 Cor. 7:36).

Jesus had said that to look with lust at a woman was "heart adultery", and marriage should lessen this temptation. Particularly in cases where husbands were prepared to lead their wives and homes in Christ-like love and protection, they should give themselves to their wives and love them as Christ loved the Church and gave up His own desires. This would certainly decrease the risk of further adulterous relationships, and women would have no problem in respecting such Christ-like husbands.

Today, many women are fiercely independent as a result of the rejection of divorce. Men are confused about their masculine role. The offspring of a generation who lost their fathers during two world wars. The fathers lost their wives' fidelity.

Conclusion

The answer is in Jesus alone, who can teach men to once again protect their wives and families in a Godly, well-ordered, Biblically, structured home
(Eph. 5:22–28).

A Marriage Floundering on the Grounds of Adultery

Little Trish, he called her.
She made his false heart sing.
The fact that he was married
Didn't mean a thing.
He had two baby daughters
He wanted to forget.
In excitement of her fond embrace,
He was entangled yet.

He came home late at night,
Leaving preaching to his wife,
Leaving little kids with other folks.
This was further strife.

One day when he was preaching,
God got through *to him* instead.
He read aloud to everyone
Proverbs 5:18, which said,
"Satisfy your strong desires,
with th' wife of your youth."
Only she is yours by right.
This is Bible truth.

C in Dys

MARRIAGEABLE ALONE AGAIN BUT NOT ALONE

This tree is dead
and buried,
though you wouldn't think it so.
So many lies and bitterness
has killed it through and through.
Its branches all are brittle,
a skeleton of a tree.
"If only" is the constant cry
from this rejected tree.

C in Dys

It's clear from many observations that the most common cause of marriage break-up is adultery. This fact can lead to violence and even murder in some cases. Many people have said to me that when a member of their family gets married, this often leads to divorce, thus hinting that it's better to have an experimental marriage. The couples may think they are having an experimental marriage, but in actual fact there is no such thing. It's almost as painful to break from living together according to how long you have been doing so, but if the marriage has been consecrated in a church setting; at least the couple may receive the backing of their church to help them stay together and follow biblical guidelines to do so.

Bible studies for couples from the start are a good idea. Most women have a natural desire for children, and men usually would love to have a son and heir to carry on their family line. At least, this was true in the past. Israeli mothers considered it a great shame if they failed to conceive. In many cases today, families criticize those who have more than two children, and abortion is common even for social reasons. These are symptoms of an unnatural society.

God told men and women to be fruitful and multiply, and a man should leave his father and his mother and cleave to his wife, not *wives*.

Virginity is a precious thing for both sexes; once it is lost, it cannot be regained.

I have referred to the sexual act, as the act of marriage, because such it should be.

Living together unwed, does not teach about true marriage.

A couple need to be convinced that they want to live together faithfully for the rest of their lives.

A couple need **to like** one another before they even think of marrying. Sexual involvement with anyone creates a soul tie, and it makes for a tearing apart when they change partners.

Fierce wrangles between couples on chat shows, illustrate what troubles families get into when partners are unfaithful. This is particularly sad where children are involved.

Church needs to come behind the couple in prayer and support them from the start. Even if a couple move to a new area a mutually agreed letter to their new church could be very useful.

If a couple moves to a new house or job because of the temptation to be unfaithful, each person has to be tough on self-nature in this treacherous situation. Jesus said a lustful look is the seed of adultery, and two looks means the seed, germinating.

Apostle Paul said he keeps his body under control, lest having preached to others, he should himself become a castaway. Joseph allowed himself to be imprisoned in order to escape the advances of his boss's wife. Fidelity in our marriages must be our utmost priority; otherwise, we'll bring ridicule on the name of Jesus and His Church. Jesus was tempted in all points like we are, yet He is without sin. We should be abiding in Him, and in this way His mighty Holy Spirit will help us to overcome temptation. I still grieve over the fact that my own marriage broke down, and I had no other option than to let him go according to the word of God, which was confirmed by my Christian solicitor.

Although I've been single again for many years, the Lord has kept me. I was married for thirty-two years. The Lord has been far better to me than a husband. I would say to anyone reading this to cry out to Him in your hour of need; He will come to your aid, and you will glorify Him.

Jesus is a fine example to us all as to how a caring partner should be. He cared for all the women in his life. He delivered them from demons, and He respected His mother's wishes at the wedding party in Cana of Galilee even though His ministry had not begun in its fuller sense. During the unimaginable agony of the cross, He spoke to His mother and gave His follower John responsibility to look after her. He understood the pain she was going through and had forewarned her that it would come, that a sword would pass through her body as it would through His.

Love covers a multitude of sins. Jesus fills up the empty spaces with His love. He heals the broken-hearted and binds up their wounds.

Write here how you overcame loneliness this week.

Where Can I Find True Love?

How do I know that he loves me?
How do I know that he cares?
How do I know that the thing he asks of me ... is really love at all?

I know some people who talk about love
that lasts a lifetime through.
But since I've never seen it in practice,
How can I say "I do", love you till death do us separate?

I've seen so many of my friends
whose love has turned to hate.
Their homes have become a battleground
with nothing to celebrate!

They fight and scrap and criticise
till there's nothing left to do
but run away and hide somewhere
until the pain abates.

How do I know that they love me?
How do I know that they care?
My brothers and sisters in sadness?
My brothers and sisters in despair?

Love That Is Real

The only thing I know right now, as I kneel at the end of my bed, Is
that Jesus went through similar pains. He didn't want to die. He said,
"Father, say there's another way to get rid of their sin and hate."
But God said, "No. You will have to go and die so
they can relate." God makes love real.

Divorce

I hate divorce, but I don't hate you.
I hate the sin that makes you weep,

that makes you mourn, that makes you cry,
that makes you walk about forlorn enough to die.

I hate the sin you often see
as you watch the worst parts of TV,
that makes them think that sin's a joke when she's off with another bloke,
leaving her faithful husband behind
to care for the kids. You'd think she'd gone blind
to leave her little family,
to follow that man she can hardly know
Who, when he's eaten and had his fill,
Will soon be off for another kill,
Lust, cruel, and hungry still!

C in Dys

PART 3

Alone Again, But, marriageable

The Bible contains deeper meanings than the English language can portray. Our understanding of the language is often seriously affected, by our experience and the culture in which we have been brought up. For these and many other reasons, the Bible teaches that we should not argue about words. But there are examples of the Apostle Paul stressing the basic truths of the Gospel. These are the reasons why I am writing *Alone Again but Marriageable*. My prayer is to dispel myths in our thinking and argue the case for one party only in a divorce situation blessed, by the Church, in a remarriage consecration. I put forward the view, that it's the church leader's task to discern, using the gifts of the Holy Spirit, who is telling the *TRUTH* and who is *NOT*, especially in a divorce situation.

Apostles had Holy Spirit promptings about certain prominent people who were telling lies to the Church, such discernment is sorely needed today if marriages are going to last for a lifetime, as God intended that they should. The Bible's author wants us to discern and obey the truth of His Word. When Jesus was tempted by the devil, He combated the half-truths with the other side of the coin of truth, We should do the same regarding divorce and remarriage, and thus put down commonly held myths that are half-truths and cause so much pain to the victims of unwarranted divorces.

Alone Again deals with the subject of the breakdown of Christian marriage (how it can happen).

It seeks to give the biblical answer to the ever-present problem of who should and should not remarry after a divorce.

Marriageable, examines how we may ensure that we now have the right attitude to marriage and are fully healed from Divorce wounds, or any relationship breakdowns. Jesus seeks a Bride without spot or wrinkle.

There is no room for lies in a marriage. A lying spirit must be, cast out, if a marriage is to survive. Marriage vows made in the Church, to a virgin bride are special in God's sight.

If the man breaks those vows at any time,

> A wife may forgive him, but if he continues in the same
> sin seventy-seven times (about two years,);

> sin is not repented of and she has no other recourse than to
> divorce him. This behaviour makes a mockery of Christianity,
> and in this modern age, from a practical level she could
> get AIDS or another sexually transmitted disease.

One of the questions asked is, "Who is most responsible when a marriage falls apart? Who is the real victim?" In other words, who is the divorcer, and who is the divorcee? The Hebrew *kerithuth* speaks of cutting off a bond, and *garish* indicates a more violent element to a divorce, similar to that of driving off an enemy. I have come to believe that a man who is regularly violent to his wife is regularly divorcing her, and she has a right to legalise this matter if he refuses to repent and stop the terrorization (Matt. 18:17).

Even when divorce is inevitable and sown into a marriage from its start, it is still a painful process because in a sense, the divorcers are cutting away their own flesh when they divorce their husbands or wives (Gen. 2:24). Even putting away a partner, as old versions of the Bible sometimes put it, it is a painful process. No one likes being rejected.

Most Christians know that God hates divorce, and many victims of divorce think that God must hate them too because in English, only one word is used for both states. I think this is the reason for much of our confusion about Jesus's words on the subject. What they do not usually realize is that it is the result of divorce that God hates.

> The tangled relationships, the confused children who don't
> feel they really belong to anyone – these are the fruits of a
> society that has lost its image of fatherhood and Christian
> family ideals. Anything goes and masquerades as a family.

All types of sexual and other sins have to be repented of in order for Christian family values to develop and Godly contentment and love to enter into homes once more (1 Tim. 6:6). In order for this to happen, the Church needs to become an example of good practice to the world, and not the reverse. It is sometimes because of discord in natural, heterosexual relationships in the home and unfaithfulness that people turn to homosexual parodies of family life. Their only image of love is sexual; they need to be close to someone, and if they have not received real affection from their parents because they are too involved with their problems and quarrels, the present climate of opinion allows people to think that they have a right to choose someone of the same sex and even build a "family" with them.

Many organisations that call themselves churches condone this unbiblical behaviour today (2 Tim. 2:22; Matt. 23:16).

Many non-believers as well as believers want to bring their families up in a healthy, moral environment. Surely it is now the Church's opportunity to apply real Christian biblical principles to its membership. In this way, when the End Time Harvest of Souls happens that many people are prophesying about today, and numerous new believers (many from broken homes) enter the Church, we will be ready for them. Church leadership therefore should be ready to exercise the tough, often confrontational love of true Church discipline when it is needed. Otherwise, it will fall away as the leaven of deceit and immorality creeps in once more and stops blessing.

Discernment of Spirits

Church leaders must be involved in divorce discernment, using all aptitudes in spiritual gifts in order for the whole Church to grow in grace and the knowledge of Christ, who alone can stabilise faltering relationships.

All marriages and Christian relationships must be built on Christ and his Word in order to survive. Also, discipline of the divorcer is essential in this process, if the Church is to share Jesus's victory.

Christ in our finances and budgeting.

Today, everything we hear and see encourages us to spend our hard-earned cash. The main motto seems to be "Freely you have received, and freely spend" instead of "like the Bible tells us to do and freely give.

A couple needs to begin **together** by giving cheerfully at least one-tenth of their joint income to the work of God, remembering that the Lord loves a cheerful giver.

Remember that God must be first, our partner next, and then our children. We must not love money or the things we can buy with it. Our children need this lesson too. Also, they need your time more than your gifts. How many marriages and families have been ruined because of a wrong focus?

The parent has spent too much time on his or her job and has missed all the precious moments of childhood. Before we know where we are, the children have grown up and moved away from us. The time is so short that we have to influence our children for good.

'Train a child up in the way he should go, and when he is grown, he will not depart from it." Time is not on our side as our children grow up. Boys in particular model themselves on their fathers, and they are influenced by their mothers in the choice of wives.

Another factor that needs to be thrashed out before marriage is how we intend to bring up our children and our thoughts on discipline.

Discipline

We need to have a biblical base for this side of marriage and parenthood. If we read carefully through the book of Proverbs, we will see a clear pattern emerging that clarifies the fact that discipline begins in childhood, and the parent is responsible for this. As the child grows older, he or she is expected to obey the parents. In recent days, this order of respect and obedience has been reversed, but we as parents need to follow Christian principles. This firmly cuts out gay anything as unbiblical, and we need to go back to the original meaning of the word *gay*, which means happy and (for we Bible believers) joyful. God bless the Evangelical Alliance for its recent stand on the matter.

We need to mentor our children in true, loving marriage between a man and a woman. We must **show them** how financial matters can be ironed out through careful and prayerful example. We must teach children to budget their own money; it's well worth it.

MARRIAGEABLE ALONE AGAIN BUT NOT ALONE

The dark depths try to hide it, where for ages trees have stood.
Others look so lush and bright as the sun comes shining through.
They reach into the sunlight with blossom fine and true.
Fruitfulness their fervent aim, to give to me and you.
But the tree behind it
Hides away in shame,
Its branches bare and lifeless,
Its roots all dead in pain.
It won't bear fruit, it's sad to say,
For things went wrong inside its roots.
It cried and screamed in pain;
Then bitterness took over,
And it bent and died again.
Don't let divorce defeat you.
Pray and pray again.
Jesus told us
We'd have strife,
But we will live again.
Let's take our cross up daily.
Let Jesus heal our pain.
He took His burden bravely,
And we must do the same.
Bitter acts may trouble us,
But we must die to pain.
For joy comes in the morning,
And everlasting gain.

CInDys

CINDYS

A home
Is not a plot of land
Where on a house is built.
A home is where
Our mem'ries are
Of Mum and Dad and kids,
Where they played and laughed and squabbled,
And wrote their little ditties,
Made their marks upon the walls as they grew and grew,
Then left us.

CInDys

<u>CinDys</u>

Christian leaders need to find out who is a divorcee and who is a divisive person. They must bring discipline to the situation.

VICTORY BLOSSOMS

This tree blossoms brightly,
sweet perfume now abounds,
Love, Joy, peace,
FRUITFULNESS!
JOY TO ALL AROUND!

Lightning Source UK Ltd.
Milton Keynes UK
UKHW01f1830270518
323300UK00001B/29/P